A CATECHISM FOR
CHRISTIAN GROWTH

190 Questions & Answers
To Strengthen the Roots of Our Faith

BENJAMIN TELLINGHUISEN

KRESS
BIBLICAL
RESOURCES

The Woodlands, Texas

A Catechism for Christian Growth

Copyright © 2023 Benjamin Tellinghuisen

Cover, Illustrations, and Graphic Design: Phoebe McCormick, phoebemccormickdesigns@gmail.com

Published by:

KRESS BIBLICAL RESOURCES

Kress Biblical Resources
The Woodlands, Texas
www.kressbiblical.com

ISBN: 978-1-934952-78-8

ENDORSEMENTS FOR
A CATECHISM FOR CHRISTIAN GROWTH

"Every recent poll teaches us that the evangelical church in the West is seriously and danger-ously lacking in basic Bible knowledge and sound theology. One solution to this problem is the proper use of Catechisms, something the church has used for centuries but which has fallen out of favor today. For this reason, I am thrilled to recommend *A Catechism for Christian Growth* for churches, families, and individuals. In fact, it is precisely what I have been looking for to give to churches, adults, and families in order to help them know and teach the great truths of Scripture and the glorious gospel of our Lord Jesus Christ. Benjamin Tellinghuisen has faithfully written this catechism to teach a new generation of Christians the truths of the Bible and faithful ortho-dox theology, something which the church desperately needs. All those who use this catechism will grow in their understanding of Scripture and Christian doctrine and even more, they will learn to rejoice, trust, and obey our sovereign and gracious triune Creator, Redeemer, and Lord."

STEPHEN J. WELLUM, *Professor of Christian Theology, The Southern Baptist Theological Seminary*

"*A Catechism for Christian Growth* provides an enriching treasure of biblical truth that is intend-ed for individual use and/or corporate use in one's natural family and in the church, i.e., one's spiritual family. May it find a fruitful future in strengthening readers' understanding of and com-mitment to God's Word!"

RICHARD MAYHUE, *author, Biblical Doctrine with John MacArthur; Research Professor of Theology Emeritus, The Master's Seminary*

"Readers should consider reading at the first glance, the final paragraph of the appendix, A Bibli-cal Rationale for Using a Catechism. The author gives—as a close to his defense of the practice of catechesis—a summary of the strengths of this practice and of this specific catechism. Ben-jamin Tellinghuisen highlights the importance of specific biblical truth (doctrinally understood) in the parent-child relationship, the husband-wife relationship, the atmosphere of personal devo-tion, the hearty participation in corporate worship, one's interaction with the unbelief and hostility of the world, the stewardship of personal callings, the enjoyment of creation, providence, and redemption, interpretation of the inspired word, and assurance that one has been found salvifi-cally by an electing, redeeming God. The presentation of the book is beautiful; its organization is attractively systematic; it is orthodox, evangelical, confessional, and clearly baptistic. The question/answer relationships are memorable. On points where Baptists might hold slight dis-agreements, the handling is fraternal. I hope thousands of churches will use this as an element of Christian instruction throughout the entire spectrum of ages in the church's stewardship of the faith once for all delivered to the saints."

TOM J. NETTLES, *Senior Professor of Historical Theology, The Southern Baptist Theological Seminary*

"As the supervisor of Benjamin Tellinghuisen's initial work on this project, I was impressed by his dedication to making Christian doctrine accessible to the members of his local church so they could live it out in practical and God-honoring ways. With this publication of *A Catechism for Christian Growth*, I'm thankful that what was a limited project is now available to God's people and their churches everywhere. If you want to embrace sound doctrine and put it into practice, this simple, clearly written, and thorough guide is indispensable!"

GREGG R. ALLISON, *Professor of Christian Theology, The Southern Baptist Theological Seminary*

"As chapters of church history have opened and closed, catechisms have been proven tools for systematizing theology and maintaining sound doctrine. Benjamin Tellinghuisen's contribution to the time-tested practice of catechizing is a welcome anchor for Christians to deepen and strengthen biblical convictions. These pages are a one-volume curriculum on the substance of the Christian faith. I'm confident this resource will bear the fruit of righteous living."

RICK HOLLAND, *Senior Pastor, Mission Road Bible Church, Kansas City, KS*

"*A Catechism for Christian Growth* is a wonderful tool for Christian discipleship. It evidences much thoughtful work, careful articulation, and rich biblical summations. The structure of beginning with the "basics" and then moving on to richer and deeper expressions of the truths of the Christian faith works very well. Individuals, families, small groups, and other communities of Christians can benefit much from reading carefully and slowly through the richness of this Catechism. May God use it mightily for the growth of His people, to the Glory of His name."

BRUCE A. WARE, *Chairman of the Department of Christian Theology, The Southern Baptist Theological Seminary*

"*A Catechism for Christian Growth* is a marvelous tool to help believers to systematically and methodically grasp key elements of the biblical message. One of its great strengths (among many) is that it can work with family devotions, a discipleship relationship, or a part of a local church service. In the face of significant confusion about biblical teaching, this catechism provides helpful content and a superb layout to make a great contribution to any Christ-follower's library and ministry."

MICHAEL A. GRISANTI, *Chair of Old Testament Department, and Distinguished Research Professor, The Master's Seminary*

"*A Catechism for Christian Growth* is done by a faithful pastor for the good of his church and it shows. It is biblical, understandable, accessible and helpful. We are definitely using this in our church!"

ROBERT B. JOHNSON, II, *Senior Pastor, Cornerstone Baptist Church, Roseville, MI*

"Planting the word deep in the heart is done well with memorable pictures that encapsulate truth. This catechism does just that, and is a must-have for family, church, and individual Christians. Benjamin provides 190 solid questions and answers that will instruct you to be grounded in the truth."

CHARLIE RAMPFUMEDZI, *President of Christ Seminary, Polokwane, South Africa*

"Benjamin Tellinghuisen has provided the church with an incredible resource for teaching a new generation the essential doctrines of the Christian faith. He has assembled a contemporary catechism steeped in the Protestant tradition to help ground believers in the faith once for all delivered to the saints. If you're a pastor seeking to catechize your church, you'll definitely want to get your hands on this excellent tool."

P. CHASE SEARS, *Assistant Professor of Biblical Studies, Southwestern Baptist Theological Seminary*

"I was looking for a like-minded catechism to assist me in my fatherly responsibility of teaching God's Word to my children and this fits perfectly. But this isn't just for kids, as a missionary who's served in the Dominican Republican and now Spain, I know it would be a great discipleship tool for churches in my Hispanic context."

JEREMIE ROY, *Missionary with Iglesia Cristiana Bautista del Valle, Alicante, Spain*

"At a time when professing Christians are susceptible to false teaching that can shipwreck their lives and leave their churches in ruin, an urgent need exists for systematic training in sound doctrine. *A Catechism for Christian Growth* is a well-crafted tool for instruction in orthodox theology and is suitable for use in the home and the church. The questions are tersely worded, supported by Scripture, baptist in perspective, and illustrated beautifully. God is already using this resource to strengthen the members of our fellowship."

DAVE MARRIOTT, *Lead Pastor, Lakewood Baptist Church, Pewaukee, WI*

CONTENTS

INTRODUCTION

Whenever I mention developing and using a catechism to mainstream evangelicals from other churches, I often get an odd look and a follow up question, "Isn't that a Catholic thing?" But far from being a machination of Rome, the use and development of a catechism is profoundly Protestant and—more importantly—biblical. The Bible teaches that all Christians must possess a rich theological framework so they can better fear, love, and worship God. Having core theological truths committed to memory is indispensable to these tasks. So, Protestants throughout the centuries have sought to faithfully train children and adults in the basics of the Christian faith through catechisms. Today, there is a growing movement to re-introduce this current generation to the faithful use of a catechism in the body-life of the church. But interest in catechism use will only gain traction among those who have been awakened to the church's great biblical responsibility of affirming, teaching, protecting, and living out—sound doctrine.

We Need to Know Sound Doctrine

Without sound doctrine derived from the Word of God there are no guard rails for morality, there are no lanes to stay in while reading and interpreting the Bible, and there is no accurate framework to think about for all of life. Everyone has a theology. Everyone has a worldview. But Christianity is designed to be a worldview based on biblically derived sound doctrine. For generations, sound doctrine has been minimized, so much so that evangelicals are as apt as liberal Christians to say, "Christianity is all about a relationship not a religion," or "Doctrine divides," or "We want good deeds, not good creeds." When sound doctrine is minimized, catechism use fades. That which used to be very Protestant now seems foreign. The remedy? Rediscover that every Christian needs to affirm, cherish, and defend sound doctrine.

Paul instructed Titus to make sure that every elder:

> hold firm to the trustworthy word as taught, so that he may be able to give instruction in sound doctrine and also to rebuke those who contradict it (Titus 1:9).

Notice, pastors are called, not just to teach the Bible, but to teach the Bible through the grid of "sound doctrine." And so, sound doctrine is designed, not just for the pastors, but for the whole church.

But what exactly is "sound doctrine?" When we break apart the phrase, we see "doctrine," as teachings that reflect the whole of Scripture's understanding on a given topic,[1] and "sound," as in healthy, good for the church, and free from error.[2] The fact that "sound," elsewhere has a more literal meaning of physically healthy gives a beautiful picture of doctrine that is both truthful and nourishing to the soul. Catechisms were simply how the church, for centuries, chose to help communicate sound doctrine.

We Need to Live Sound Doctrine

Paul also makes clear to Timothy that sound doctrine is not a set of obscure statements for the initiated to contemplate as they grow disconnected from everyday life. Instead, sound doctrine nourishes the soul and promotes godly living. Paul repeatedly made the connection from his faithful life to his sound doctrine, writing to Timothy while in prison:

> Follow the pattern of the sound words that you have heard from me, in the faith and love that are in Christ Jesus (2 Tim 1:13).

That Paul could point to a "pattern" of "faith and love" for Timothy to follow, shows us that sound doctrine reverberated in his life. In 1 Timothy 6, not only did Paul write about "sound teaching that accords with godliness" (godly living), but he also warned that "different doctrines" fuel all sorts of godlessness.

> If anyone teaches a different doctrine and does not agree with the sound words of our Lord Jesus Christ and the teaching that accords with godliness, he is puffed up with conceit and understands nothing. He has an unhealthy craving for controversy and for quarrels about words, which produce envy, dissension, slander, evil suspicions, and constant friction among people who are depraved in mind and deprived of the truth, imagining that godliness is a means of gain (1 Tim 6:3-5).

False doctrines produce pride and all sorts of wicked fruit, whereas sound doctrine yields that which is honoring to God. That is why in the quintessential passage on discipleship in the New Testament (Titus 2), Paul prefaced a whole series of commands to help one another pursue godly living with a primary and unifying framework:

> But as for you, teach what accords with sound doctrine. (Titus 2:1)

The pursuit, knowledge, and protection of sound doctrine is essential to how God calls every Christian to live the Christian life. One might say, "Good creeds are for good deeds." The backbone for why the Scriptures support the use of a well-crafted catechism is simply that catechisms are excellent tools to communicate, learn, and study—sound doctrine.

Since reciting *A Catechism for Christian Growth* in the services of our church, I could cite several examples of God using the *CCG* to protect, strengthen, and encourage church members' faith. One such example occurred the week after we recited catechism question 104, "Can we separate repentance and saving faith? No, repentance and faith are inseparable experiences of God's grace because saving faith is always a repentant faith. We cannot truly believe without turning from sin and we cannot truly turn from sin without believing (Mark 1:15; Luke 9:23)." A few days after reciting this at church, a church member's friend told him that he had believed in Jesus when he was young, but still wasn't ready to give up living his sinful lifestyle. The friend was a drunkard and enjoyed multiple sexual partners, all while saying he loved Jesus too. The church member quickly pulled out the catechism statement and verses still folded in his Bible and helped him see the truth of God's sound doctrine on repentance and faith. Sound doctrine is essential to godly living and catechisms propel us toward that goal.

How A Catechism for Christian Growth Helps

Despite what some might think, catechisms are not simply tools for children (though I know every Christian child will benefit from learning a biblical catechism). Catechisms are for every Christian to learn sound doctrine. *A Catechism for Christian Growth* has been developed to be useful for everyone, from toddlers to pastors who want to refresh their theology.

But, with such venerable catechisms available, like the *Westminster Catechism,* the *Heidelberg Catechism,* and for Baptists, *Keach's Baptist Catechism* and even *Spurgeon's Catechism,* why is there a need to write a new catechism? Interestingly enough, even these classic catechisms were developed to meet specific needs when they were written. In fact, new catechisms were developed up until the early 20th century. Thankfully, we've seen a renewed interest in the use of catechisms today and a couple new catechisms have been developed and well-received in recent years. Still, the question remains. Why *A Catechism for Christian Growth?*

For many Christians, a perennial weakness is fitting the whole storyline of Scriptures together, discerning how each passage integrates into Christian theology. The *CCG* provides that framework in a way that many other catechisms do not. In Bible teaching churches we are taught to read our Bibles and pray, but reading the Bible without a theological framework often results in a hodge-podge of related truths rather than a neat and tidy scaffold built on God's Word. Since most systematic theology books are inaccessible to the average Christian, the *CCG* provides a helpful foundation for the rich theological tradition we've inherited over the last 2,000 years. So, to accommodate the development of language, the development of biblical and theological studies, and to reintroduce a new generation to the idea of catechism, I have developed, *A Catechism for Christian Growth: 190 Questions and Answers to Strengthen the Roots of our Faith.*

A couple of notes to keep in mind as you work through the catechism:
- Note the structure of the *CCG* in the Table of Contents. It is specifically designed to walk through the major points of theology.
- Try to read through the catechism in a single sitting or two to get the full picture.
- The *CCG* is designed to grow with a family. The catechism includes a 20-question foundation, perfect for younger children (the 20 questions are part of the full 190).
  - » There is also a one-year rotation of 52 questions noted by a leaf sign. These are perfect for reciting weekly in a church service, using in children's or youth ministry classes, or simply as a discipleship tool for new believers.
  - » The answers designed to be memorized first are in **bold font**, but longer answers are included to clarify and aid in your personal study of various topics.
- As you work on memorization, always repeat the question when you give the answer, so the question too is committed to memory.
- Work on memorizing sections that feel less familiar to you.
- Consider memorizing the Scriptures quoted after each question as part of your Scripture memory regimen.
- Incorporate catechism review into your daily devotion time.

- Notes on theological convictions:
  - » The *CCG* is thoroughly Protestant and is based on the rich Protestant tradition of catechetical instruction. Several historic catechisms were used in the construction of the *CCG* and those citations are found in the end notes.
  - » The *CCG* is designed for those who believe in and practice believer's baptism.
  - » A few additional answers are given throughout the book, so that Christians with differing theological convictions will still find the catechism immediately useable.
- As one of my seminary professors used to say, "Theology is life." So, always approach the catechism expecting God to make the truths that you learn imminently applicable to your life.

I'd like to thank my children for years of faithfully working through Daddy's catechism in all its different formats. Eli, Abigail, and Esther, this is my labor of love for you. I'd also like to thank my beloved church family, First Baptist Church of Farmington, for their ongoing love and support, zeal for God's Word, and embrace of the *CCG*. I couldn't have developed the book in the form you hold in your hands without Phoebe McCormick who collaborated with me in both the artwork and design of the book and my doctoral advisors and many subsequent readers who helped me edit and refine the catechism over the last four years. Thank you all for your hard work. Lastly, and most importantly, I'd like to thank my beloved wife Leah who has supported me through years of classes, research trips, and all the joys and trials of ministry. Soli Deo Gloria.

Benjamin Tellinghuisen – January 2023

---

[1] Klaus Wegenast, "*didaskalia*," in NIDNTT, ed. Colin Brown, 3: 768-771 (Grand Rapids: Zondervan, 1986), 770. "Sound doctrine" as a summary or systematized set of doctrinal truths is most clearly developed in the pastoral epistles.

[2] Walter Bauer, W. F. Arndt, F. W. Gingrich, and F. W. Danker, *A Greek-English Lexicon of the New Testament and other Early Christian Literature*, 3rd ed., ed. F. W. Danker (Chicago: The University of Chicago Press, 2000), 1023.

20 QUESTION
FOUNDATION

1 What is the chief purpose of humanity?

To glorify God and enjoy him forever.

2 What is our only hope in life and death?

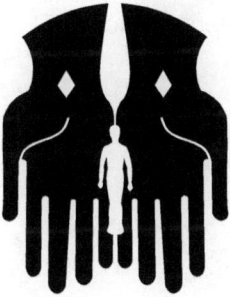

That we are not our own but belong to God.

3 Can we belong to God apart from Christ?

No one comes to the Father, except through Christ alone.

4 What is the Word of God?

The Bible is the Word of God and our sufficient guide for all of life.

5 What does the Bible teach?

The whole Bible centers on the gospel message.

6 What is God?

God is the creator, sustainer, and ruler of everyone and everything.

7   Who is the one true God?

The one true God eternally exists in three persons: God the Father, God the Son, and God the Holy Spirit.

8   What does it mean that God is holy?

God is sinless in every way and set apart above all creation.

9   What makes humanity special?

God created us in his own image to know, glorify, and enjoy him forever.

10 If we are made in God's image, why is there sin and death?

Adam and Eve disobeyed God in the garden. Instead of holy and happy, they became sinful and miserable.

11 What are the effects of this first sin on us?

We are all born in sin and guilt and therefore unable to glorify and enjoy God.

12 How can we escape punishment and belong to God?

God himself, as a loving Father, delivers us from the power and penalty of sin by a Redeemer.

13   Who is the Redeemer?

The only Redeemer is the Lord Jesus Christ, the eternal Son of God.

14   What is the final hope of our salvation?

To be given a glorified body and dwell in the presence of God forever.

15   What is prayer?

Prayer is pouring out the desires of our hearts to God.

16 How should we feel about those who have not trusted in Jesus?

Our hearts should mourn and grow with compassion towards all unbelievers.

17 What is the goal of evangelism?

To make lifelong disciples of Jesus Christ.

18 How can we worship God?

By glorifying and enjoying him in everything we do.

19   Where is Christ now?

He rose physically from the dead and is now seated at the right hand of the Father.

20   What is Christ doing in heaven?

He upholds the universe and intercedes for us.

THE BIG PICTURE

1 What is the chief purpose of humanity?

To glorify God and enjoy him forever (1 Cor. 10:31; Ps 73:25-26).

Psalm 73:25–26
Whom have I in heaven but you?
And there is nothing on earth that I desire besides you.
My flesh and my heart may fail,
but God is the strength of my heart and my portion forever.

2 What is our only hope in life and death?

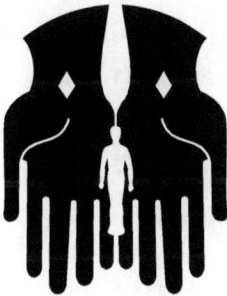

That we are not our own but belong, body and soul, both in life and death, **to God** and to our Savior Jesus Christ (Rom 14:7-9; 1 Cor 6:19-20; 1 Thess 5:9-10).

Romans 14:7-9
For none of us lives to himself, and none of us dies to himself. For if we live, we live to the Lord, and if we die, we die to the Lord. So then, whether we live or whether we die, we are the Lord's. For to this end Christ died and lived again, that he might be Lord both of the dead and of the living.

---

* The leaf symbol notes that it belongs to the 52-question rotation of the *CCG*.

3 What does it mean to belong to God?

To belong to God is **to be forgiven of sin, adopted into God's eternal family, and united to Christ by faith** alone through God's grace alone (Eph 1:5-10; Gal 2:20-21; John 1:12).

John 1:12
But to all who did receive him, who believed in his name, he gave the right to become children of God,

4 Can we belong to God apart from Christ?

No one comes to the Father, except through Christ alone (John 14:6).

John 14:6
Jesus said to him, "I am the way, and the truth, and the life. No one comes to the Father except through me."

5 How do we know there is a God?

All creation proclaims there must be a Creator, and all humanity has a sense of morality and eternity imprinted within them by the Creator; **but the Word of God alone fully reveals** the one true **God and tells us how we can belong to him** (Rom 1:19-20; Ps 19; Eccl 3:11).

Romans 1:19-20
For what can be known about God is plain to them, because God has shown it to them. For his invisible attributes, namely, his eternal power and divine nature, have been clearly perceived, ever since the creation of the world, in the things that have been made. So they are without excuse.

THE WORD OF GOD

6 What is the Word of God?

The Bible is the Word of God and our sufficient guide to teach, correct, and train **for all of life** (2 Pet 1:3; 2 Tim 3:16-17).

2 Timothy 3:16-17
All Scripture is breathed out by God and profitable for teaching, for reproof, for correction, and for training in righteousness, that the man of God may be complete, equipped for every good work.

7 What does the Bible teach?

The Bible reveals the one true God, explains what is wrong with the world, and tells how we can be right with and belong to God forever. **The whole Bible centers on the gospel message**, making us wise for salvation (2 Tim 3:14-15; Eccl 12:13).

2 Timothy 3:14-15
But as for you, continue in what you have learned and have firmly believed, knowing from whom you learned it and how from childhood you have been acquainted with the sacred writings, which are able to make you wise for salvation through faith in Christ Jesus.

8 What is the significance of calling Jesus the Word?

Jesus perfectly reveals God in the flesh, and through Christ alone we are made right with God and can belong to God forever (John 1:1, 14; Luke 24:27).

John 1:1
In the beginning was the Word, and the Word was with God, and the Word was God.

9 Who wrote the Bible?

Men inspired by the Holy Spirit wrote the Bible using the language and style with which they were most familiar (2 Pet 1:20-21).

2 Peter 1:21
For no prophecy was ever produced by the will of man, but men spoke from God as they were carried along by the Holy Spirit.

10 What does it mean that the Bible is inspired?

It means the Holy Spirit moved the writers of Scripture to write all that God desired—and so the Bible is God-breathed—or inspired. Every word in the original documents is exactly as God intended it to be (John 14:26; 2 Tim 3:16; 2 Pet 1:20-21).

2 Peter 1:20
knowing this first of all, that no prophecy of Scripture comes from someone's own interpretation.

11 Since men were involved in writing the Bible, is it without error?

Yes. Since the Bible is inspired, it is inerrant and wholly true, reflecting the truthful nature of God (Heb 6:17-18; John 17:17; 1 Thess 2:13).

John 17:17
Sanctify them in the truth; your word is truth.

12 To what extent is the Bible authoritative for our lives?

We are to believe and obey God's Word in everything it addresses, **as if God Himself spoke directly to us** (1 Thess 2:13; 2 Thess 2:15; 3:14; 2 Pet 3:15-16).

2 Thessalonians 3:14
If anyone does not obey what we say in this letter, take note of that person, and have nothing to do with him, that he may be ashamed.

13 Do we need the Bible in order to belong to God?

Yes. The Bible is necessary to know God's gospel, to grow in holiness, and to discern how to glorify and enjoy God both in this life and for all eternity (Rom 10:17; Matt 4:4; 1 Pet 2:2-3).

Matthew 4:4
But he answered, "It is written, 'Man shall not live by bread alone, but by every word that comes from the mouth of God.'"

14 Is the Bible still relevant today?

Yes. The Scriptures are clear and remain relevant for Christians today, revealing truth about God and ourselves. Therefore, the Bible should be translated carefully into every language (Deut 29:29; Col 3:16; Heb 4:12).

Deuteronomy 29:29
The secret things belong to the LORD our God, but the things that are revealed belong to us and to our children forever, that we may do all the words of this law.

15 How many books are there in the Bible?

There are 39 books in the Old Testament and 27 books in the New Testament, for a total of 66 books. Jesus affirmed the divine authority of the Old Testament and promised the inspiration of the New Testament (Luke 24:44; John 16:13-14; 2 Pet 3:15-16).

Luke 24:44
Then he said to them, "These are my words that I spoke to you while I was still with you, that everything written about me in the Law of Moses and the Prophets and the Psalms must be fulfilled."

16 What are the books of the Old Testament?

The Mosaic books are: **Genesis, Exodus, Leviticus, Numbers, Deuteronomy.**

The historical books are: **Joshua, Judges, Ruth, 1 and 2 Samuel, 1 and 2 Kings, 1 and 2 Chronicles, Ezra, Nehemiah, Esther.**

The poetical books are: **Job, Psalms, Proverbs, Ecclesiastes, Song of Solomon.**

The major prophets are: **Isaiah, Jeremiah, Lamentations, Ezekiel, Daniel.**

The twelve minor prophets are: **Hosea, Joel, Amos, Obadiah, Jonah, Micah, Nahum, Habakkuk, Zephaniah, Haggai, Zechariah, Malachi.**

17 What are the books of the New Testament?

The gospels are: **Matthew, Mark, Luke, John.**

The story of the early church is: **Acts.**

Paul's letters are: **Romans, 1 and 2 Corinthians, Galatians, Ephesians, Philippians, Colossians, 1 and 2 Thessalonians, 1 and 2 Timothy, Titus, Philemon.**

The general letters are: **Hebrews, James, 1 and 2 Peter, 1, 2, and 3 John, Jude.**

The book of prophecy is: **Revelation.**

18 Should anyone add to or take from the Bible?

No, not a single word. No person, prophet, or angel has authority to add to or take from the Scriptures (Deut 4:2; Prov 30:6; Rev 22:18-19).

Proverbs 30:6
Do not add to his words, lest he rebuke you and you be found a liar.

19 Can we trust that the Bible has remained unchanged?

Yes. The Word of God promises it will remain forever. Further, we have an abundance of ancient documents that demonstrate God's preservation of the Bible in the original languages with few significant variations (Isa 40:6-8; Matt 5:18).

Matthew 5:18
For truly, I say to you, until heaven and earth pass away, not an iota, not a dot, will pass from the Law until all is accomplished.

20 How should we interpret the Bible?

We must always aim for the author's intent, taking into account the grammar, literary context, and flow of redemptive history for each passage. **Additionally, Scripture helps interpret Scripture** since God is the author of it all and cannot contradict himself (2 Pet 1:20-21; Acts 15:14-18).

2 Peter 1:20-21
knowing this first of all, that no prophecy of Scripture comes from someone's own interpretation. For no prophecy was ever produced by the will of man, but men spoke from God as they were carried along by the Holy Spirit.

21 Can we trust the Genesis account of the beginning?

Yes. Genesis 1-11, like the rest of the Bible, **presents historical facts and should be trusted completely, just as Jesus did** (Matt 19:4-5; 24:37-39).

Matthew 19:4-5
He answered, "Have you not read that he who created them from the beginning made them male and female, and said, 'Therefore a man shall leave his father and his mother and hold fast to his wife, and the two shall become one flesh'?"

GOD

22 What is God?

God is the creator, sustainer, and ruler of everyone and everything. He is eternal spirit, infinite and unchangeable in his power and perfections—his goodness and glory (Pss 24:1; 90:2; John 4:24; 1 Tim 1:17; Jas 1:17).

Psalm 24:1
The earth is the LORD's and the fullness thereof, the world and those who dwell therein.

23 Is there more than one God?

No. There is only one God and he alone is to be worshiped and feared. He tells us that his name is Yahweh (Jer 10:10; Deut 6:4; Exod 3:14-15).

Jeremiah 10:10
But Yahweh is the true God; he is the living God and the everlasting King. At his wrath the earth quakes, and the nations cannot endure his indignation.

24 Who is the one true God?

The one true God eternally exists in three persons: God the Father, God the Son, and God the Holy Spirit. These three are one God, the same in essence, and equal in power and glory (2 Cor 13:14; Matt 28:19).

Matthew 28:19
Go therefore and make disciples of all nations, baptizing them in the name of the Father and of the Son and of the Holy Spirit.

25 If there is only one God, why name three persons?

God's Word reveals the Father is God, the Son is God, and the Holy Spirit is God. **Without three persons, God is not God**, nor is he eternally self-sufficient (1 Cor 8:6; Heb 1:3; Acts 5:3-4).

1 Corinthians 8:6
yet for us there is one God, the Father, from whom are all things and for whom we exist, and one Lord, Jesus Christ, through whom are all things and through whom we exist.

26 Is God dependent on creation for anything?

No. Because God is Triune, he is totally independent and sufficient within himself to possess and enjoy the full complement of his attributes, including relational attributes, such as love. And yet, God is glorified by and derives joy from his creation (Acts 17:24-25; John 17:5, 24; 1 John 4:8, 13-16).

Acts 17:24-25
The God who made the world and everything in it, being Lord of heaven and earth, does not live in temples made by man, nor is he served by human hands, as though he needed anything, since he himself gives to all mankind life and breath and everything.

27 Does each person in the Trinity differ in their roles?

Yes. Each person of the Trinity carries out the one work of God distinctly and is uniquely involved in creating, sustaining, and saving creation. And yet, the three operate inseparably in all divine works: the Father originates through the Son by the Spirit (Gen 1:1-2; John 15:26; 2 Cor 13:14; Col 1:3-20).

2 Corinthians 13:14
The grace of the Lord Jesus Christ and the love of God and the fellowship of the Holy Spirit be with you all.

28 How does the Nicene Creed help us understand the Trinity?

It clarifies the eternal relations of the Father, Son, and Spirit in this way:

> "**We believe in one God, the Father** Almighty, **Maker of heaven and earth**, of all things visible and invisible.

> "**And we believe in one Lord Jesus Christ, the on-ly-begotten Son of God**, begotten of his Father before all time; God of God, Light of Light, true God of true God; **begotten, not made**, being of one substance with the Father, **by Whom all things were made;** who, for us men and for our salvation, came down from heaven, and was incarnate by the Holy Spirit of the virgin Mary, and was made man; and was crucified also for us under Pontius Pilate; he suffered and was buried; and the third day he rose again, according to the Scriptures; and as-cended into heaven, and is seated at the right hand of the Father; and he shall come again, with glory, to judge both the living and the dead; whose kingdom shall have no end.

> "**And we believe in the Holy Spirit, the Lord and giver of life; who proceeds from the Father and the Son;** who is worshiped and glorified together with the Father and Son, and who spoke by the prophets." (Gal 4:4-6; Heb 1:1-3; John 15:26).

29   Can God be fully known?

No. Even though God graciously reveals himself to us, **our limited minds cannot fully know the greatness of his persons and perfections** (Job 36:26; Ps 145:3; Isa 55:8-9; 1 Cor 2:11).

Psalm 145:3
Great is the LORD, and greatly to be praised, and his greatness is unsearchable.

30   If we cannot fully know God, why should we try to know him at all?

Because our highest boast is that we know the inexhaustible God; **the more we know God the more we are able to glorify and enjoy him** (Jer 9:23-24; Col 1:10; Ps 139:17-18; Phil 3:10).

Psalm 139:17-18
How precious to me are your thoughts, O God! How vast is the sum of them! If I would count them, they are more than the sand. I awake, and I am still with you.

31 Does God change his mind or make mistakes?

No. God is an eternal and perfect being and has no variation or shadow due to change. But still, God responds to our prayers and encourages us amid our trials (Jas 1:17; Ps 102:26-27; Isa 46:9-10).

James 1:17
Every good gift and every perfect gift is from above, coming down from the Father of lights, with whom there is no variation or shadow due to change.

32 Where is God?

God is omnipresent and everywhere equally, not contained by physical space. Still, his presence can have different functions, like blessing in heaven and punishing in hell (Ps 139:7-10; Amos 9:1-4; Deut 10:14).

Psalm 139:7-8
Where shall I go from your Spirit? Or where shall I flee from your presence? If I go up to the heavens, you are there; if I make my bed in the depths, you are there.

33   What does God know?

God is omniscient and therefore **knows all that is, was, will be, and could be.** He knows the secrets of our hearts, and nothing escapes his notice (1 John 3:20; Heb 4:13; Isa 46:9-10).

Hebrews 4:13
And no creature is hidden from his sight, but all are naked and exposed to the eyes of him to whom we must give account.

34   What does it mean that God is holy?

God is perfectly pure, **sinless in every way,** transcendent, **and set apart,** highly exalted **above all creation** (1 Sam 2:2; Isa 6:3; Hab 1:13; Lev 16:2).

1 Samuel 2:2
There is none holy like the Lord: for there is none besides you; there is no rock like our God.

35   Is God always just to punish evil?

Yes. God's wrath is justly poured out against all sin. He is always righteous and therefore his judgments are always just. He alone is the standard and arbiter of absolute justice (Deut 32:4; Ps 98:9; Isa 10:1-4; 45:19).

Psalm 98:9
before the Lord, for he comes to judge the earth. He will judge the world with righteousness, and the peoples with equity.

36   But isn't God merciful, withholding his wrath?

Yes. He has mercy on whom he wills, is slow to anger, and abounds in steadfast love. His mercy is a common grace gift to humanity as he allows the rain to fall on the just and the unjust, **patiently withholding his wrath until the due time** (Exod 33:19; 34:6; Matt 5:45; 1 Cor 4:5).

Exodus 34:6
The LORD passed before him and proclaimed, "The LORD, the LORD, a God merciful and gracious, slow to anger, and abounding in steadfast love and faithfulness,"

37 Does God have a primary attribute?

No. At all times God is all of his attributes; no one attribute ranks before another. **Therefore, he is perfectly just and angry while simultaneously merciful and loving.** His hatred of sin and love for humanity unite most vividly at the cross of Jesus Christ (Exod 34:6-7; Isa 53:4-6; Rom 3:23-26).

Romans 3:23-24
for all have sinned and fall short of the glory of God, and are justified by his grace as a gift, through the redemption that is in Christ Jesus,

38 How did God create all things?

God created all things out of nothing by speaking them into existence. He created the entire universe and everything within the universe, both physical and spiritual, in six consecutive days. **In the beginning, all of his creation was very good and untainted by sin** (Gen 1; Col 1:16-17; Heb 11:3).

Hebrews 11:3
By faith we understand that the universe was created by the word of God, so that what is seen was not made out of things that are visible.

39 Does God reign over his creation?

Yes. The entirety of creation is upheld by his power, from the weather to the worst of sinners. Nothing and **no one can act outside of his sovereign control** (Ps 24:1; Heb 1:3; Rev 19:16).

Hebrews 1:3
He is the radiance of the glory of God and the exact imprint of his nature, and he upholds the universe by the word of his power.

40 Why call God sovereign?

Because he is king over all, with limitless power and authority to reign over his creation, **he is able to do whatever he desires** according to his holy and perfect will (Ps 103:19; Matt 19:26).

Psalm 103:19
The LORD has established his throne in the heavens, and his kingdom rules over all.

41 What is the providence of God?

It is God's personal and powerful work, guiding all creation **to fulfill all his purposes for his glory and the good of his children** (Gen 50:20; Prov 19:21; Matt 10:29-31; John 9:1-3; Rom 8:28).

Proverbs 19:21
Many are the plans in the mind of a man, but it is the purpose of the LORD that will stand.

42 How does knowing God's sovereignty and providence encourage us?

It encourages us to be patient in adversity and thankful in prosperity, resting our highest hope in God our Father. We can be sure that there is nothing which can take us out of his faithful love, for he is the only Lord of all (Job 1:21; Rom 5:3-5; 1 Thess 5:16-18; Rom 8:38-39).

Job 1:21
And he said, "Naked I came from my mother's womb, and naked shall I return. The LORD gave, and the LORD has taken away; blessed be the name of the LORD."

CREATED THINGS
- HUMANITY - SIN

43 What makes humanity special?

God created us in his own image with the capacity **to know, glorify, and enjoy him forever.** We alone are like God and we alone can represent God (Gen 1:26-27; Isa 43:7).

Genesis 1:27
So God created man in his own image, in the image of God he created him; male and female he created them.

44 Is our gender part of God's good creation?

Yes. God created us, his image bearers, **as male and female. This means all men and all women have dignity** and significance **before God and before one another.** It also means we are to treat all people with respect and love, avoiding any sense of superiority and inferiority (Gen 1:27; Gal 3:27-29).

Galatians 3:27-28
For as many of you as were baptized into Christ have put on Christ. There is neither Jew nor Greek, there is neither slave nor free, there is no male and female, for you are all one in Christ Jesus.

45   What is marriage?

Marriage is God's ongoing gift to humanity, always defined as the union of one man and one woman. Any attempt to subvert this definition, separate sexual intimacy from marriage, or reject God's gift of biological gender rebels against God's good design (Gen 2:18, 23-24; 1 Cor 7:2; Rom 1:26-28).

Genesis 2:18, 24
Then the LORD God said, "It is not good that the man should be alone; I will make him a helper fit for him." ...Therefore a man shall leave his father and his mother and hold fast to his wife, and they shall become one flesh.

46   How should we think of singleness?

Singleness is a season of life for all human beings and is to be lived in purity. To some people God grants the gift of singleness so they may follow him with undivided attention and service (1 Cor 7:6-9, 32-35).

1 Corinthians 7:8
To the unmarried and the widows I say that it is good for them to remain single, as I am.

47   What is God's purpose for humanity?

Beginning with Adam and Eve, **God wants us to fill the earth, work, worship, and enjoy him.** He also wants us to be conformed to the image of his Son (Gen 1:28; 2:15; 2 Cor 3:18).

2 Corinthians 3:18
And we all, with unveiled face, beholding the glory of the Lord, are being transformed into the same image from one degree of glory to another. For this comes from the Lord who is the Spirit.

48   Are our physical bodies important to God?

Yes. God created us as the good and blessed **union of soul and body.** To harm the body or dismiss the physical realities of eternal life is to ignore God's good purpose and hope for all creation (Ps 139:13-16; Gen 9:5; Rom 8:23).

Romans 8:23
And not only the creation, but we ourselves, who have the firstfruits of the Spirit, groan inwardly as we wait eagerly for adoption as sons, the redemption of our bodies.

49 Is hatred or murder ever acceptable?

No. All acts that take away human life, either in the womb—abortion, **or at the end of life**—euthanasia, **are strictly forbidden.** So too is any hatred of our fellow man for any reason, especially related to differences in ethnicity, culture, age, or gender (Matt 5:21-22; Exod 21:22-25).

Matthew 5:21-22a
You have heard that it was said to those of old, 'You shall not murder; and whoever murders will be liable to judgment.' But I say to you that everyone who is angry with his brother will be liable to judgment;

50 What other creatures did God create to serve him?

God created angels to continually serve him. But some angels, led by Satan, rebelled against God (Ezek 1:4-28; 28:12-18; Jude 6; Rev 5:6-14; 12:4).

Jude 6
And the angels who did not stay within their own position of authority, but left their proper dwelling, he has kept in eternal chains under gloomy darkness until the judgment of the great day —

51 If we are made in God's image, why is there sin and death?

Adam and Eve disobeyed God in the garden by eating the forbidden fruit, succumbing to Satan's temptation. **Instead of holy and happy, they became sinful and miserable**, were cast out of the garden, and eventually died (Gen 3:14-24; Jas 1:14-15).

James 1:14–15
But each person is tempted when he is lured and enticed by his own desire. Then desire when it has conceived gives birth to sin, and sin when it is fully grown brings forth death.

52 What are the effects of this first sin on us?

We are all born in sin and guilt, spiritually dead, inheritors of a sinful nature **and therefore unable to glorify and enjoy God** (Rom 3:23; 5:12-19; Eph 2:1-3; Ps 51:5).

Romans 5:12
Therefore, just as sin came into the world through one man, and death through sin, and so death spread to all men because all sinned—

53 How can we glorify and enjoy God?

By loving him, trusting him, and obeying his commands and law (Deut 11:8-9; Col 3:9-11; 1 John 5:3).

1 John 5:3
For this is the love of God, that we keep his commandments. And his commandments are not burdensome.

54 What does the law of God require?

Perfect and perpetual obedience: **that we love the Lord our God with all our heart, soul, mind, and strength, and love our neighbor as ourselves** (Jas 2:10; Matt 5:48; 22:37-40; Rom 13:8-10).

James 2:10
For whoever keeps the whole law but fails in one point has become guilty of all of it.

55 What is the summary of the law stated in the 10 commandments, and how are they divided?

One: You shall have no other gods before me

Two: You shall not make any idols

Three: You shall not misuse the name of the LORD your God

Four: Remember the Sabbath day and keep it holy

Five: Honor your father and your mother

Six: You shall not murder

Seven: You shall not commit adultery

Eight: You shall not steal

Nine: You shall not lie

Ten: You shall not covet

Generally speaking, **the first four instruct us how to love God; the last six, how to love one another** (Exod 20:3-17; Deut 10:12-13,19)

56 As we relate to God, does God primarily regard our religious acts, or the heart behind our worship?

God is righteously angry when we honor him with our lips while our hearts are far from him (Isa 29:13; Matt 15:8).

Matthew 15:8
This people honors me with their lips, but their heart is far from me;

57 As we relate to one another, does God ONLY regard right actions, or also the heart behind those actions?

God is always most concerned with the heart. So, he warns us that the heart is deceitful above all things and desperately wicked, and therefore the root of all evil. Jesus clearly stated that murder stems from a heart of anger and adultery from a heart of lust (Jer 17:9; Matt 5:21-22, 27-28).

Jeremiah 17:9
The heart is deceitful above all things, and desperately sick; who can understand it?

58 Can anyone keep the law of God perfectly?

Since the fall, no mere **human has been able to keep the law of God perfectly.** Instead, we are prone to hating God and our neighbors (Rom 3:10, 23; 1 John 1:8, 10).

1 John 1:8
If we say we have no sin, we deceive ourselves, and the truth is not in us.

59 Since no one can keep the law, what is its purpose?

That we may know the holy nature of God, the sinful nature of our hearts, and thus our need of a Savior. The law reveals God's good standard of perfection that promotes human flourishing (Rom 3:20; Gal 3:24; Rom 7:7).

Romans 3:20
For by works of the law no human being will be justified in his sight, since through the law comes knowledge of sin.

60 What is sin?

Sin is not thinking or saying, not being or doing what God requires in his law. The root of all sin is the truth of God not sought, the holiness of God not reverenced, **the promises of God not trusted**, the wrath of God not feared, **and the person of God not loved** (1 John 3:4; Heb 11:6; Nah 1:2; Rom 1:18).

Hebrews 11:6
And without faith it is impossible to please him, for whoever would draw near to God must believe that he exists and that he rewards those who seek him.

61 What is idolatry?

Idolatry is trusting in or worshipping, **created things rather than the Creator for our hope and happiness, significance and security** (Rom 1:21, 25; Col 3:5).

Colossians 3:5
Put to death therefore what is earthly in you: sexual immorality, impurity, passion, evil desire, and covetousness, which is idolatry.

62 Will God allow our sin and idolatry to go unpunished?

No. God is righteously angry, and his holiness demands that no sin go unpunished. Therefore, his pure justice determines that **the wages of sin is both death and eternal condemnation in hell** (Rom 6:23; Eph 5:5-6; Matt 25:46).

Romans 6:23
For the wages of sin is death, but the free gift of God is eternal life in Christ Jesus our Lord.

63 Are we able to satisfy God's justice by our good works?

Not at all. No matter how many good works we do, we increase our sin and debt to God every day. Even the good we do is as filthy rags before our Holy God (Matt 6:12; Isa 64:6; Eph 2:8-9).

Isaiah 64:6
We have all become like one who is unclean, and all our righteous deeds are like a polluted garment. We all fade like a leaf, and our iniquities, like the wind, take us away.

64 How can we escape punishment and belong to God?

God himself, as a loving Father, graciously reconciles us to himself, and **delivers us from the power and penalty of sin by a Redeemer** (Isa 53:10-11; Rom 5:21).

Isaiah 53:11
Out of the anguish of his soul he shall see and be satisfied; by his knowledge shall the righteous one, my servant, make many to be accounted righteous, and he shall bear their iniquities.

GOD THE FATHER

65 Who is God the Father?

He is God, coeternal with the Son and the Holy Spirit. As the first person of the Trinity, **all creation comes from him and exists to bring him glory** (1 Cor 8:6; Eph 4:6; John 3:16; 14:16).

Ephesians 4:6
one God and Father of all, who is over all and through all and in all.

66 How does God the Father love us?

He loved us before the foundation of the world and showed us his love most fully by giving the Son as Redeemer and sending the Spirit to seal our adoption as sons and daughters (Eph 1:4-6; John 17:24-26; Gal 4:4-6).

Galatians 4:4-6
But when the fullness of time had come, God sent forth his Son, born of woman, born under the law, to redeem those who were under the law, so that we might receive adoption as sons. And because you are sons, God has sent the Spirit of his Son into our hearts, crying, "Abba! Father!"

GOD THE SON

67 Who is the Redeemer?

The only Redeemer is the Lord Jesus Christ, the eternal Son of God. He alone purchased us with his blood and brought us back to God (1 Tim 2:5-6; 1 Cor 6:19-20).

1 Timothy 2:5–6
For there is one God, and there is one mediator between God and men, the man Christ Jesus, who gave himself as a ransom for all, which is the testimony given at the proper time.

68 What sort of Redeemer is needed to bring us back to God?

One who is truly human and also truly God, coeternal with the Father and the Holy Spirit. He is like us in every respect, yet without sin, and at the same time never gave up his divinity, always upholding the universe by the Word of his power (Col 2:9; Heb 4:15; 1:3).

Hebrews 4:15
For we do not have a high priest who is unable to sympathize with our weaknesses, but one who in every respect has been tempted as we are, yet without sin.

69 Why must the Redeemer be truly human?

First, to obey God's law which we could never obey. **Second, to physically die, suffering the punishment for sin** which we could never endure. Thus, he is fully able to sympathize with our weakness and comfort us in our moments of need (Heb 2:14, 17; 4:15; Rom 5:17).

Hebrews 2:17
Therefore he had to be made like his brothers in every respect, so that he might become a merciful and faithful high priest in the service of God, to make propitiation for the sins of the people.

70 Why must the Redeemer be truly God?

First, to endure God's wrath poured out for the sins of humanity. **Second, to restore righteousness** and eternal life **which we lost at the Fall.** Thus, he is fully able to save the elect (1 Pet 3:18; 1 John 2:1-2; Acts 2:24; 1 John 4:9-10).

1 Peter 3:18
For Christ also suffered once for sins, the righteous for the unrighteous, that he might bring us to God, being put to death in the flesh but made alive in the spirit,

71 How did God the Son become man?

He was supernaturally conceived by the Holy Spirit and born of the virgin Mary, so as to be of two natures, yet not inherit the sin of Adam. **This is called the incarnation.** He grew naturally and was perfectly dependent on the Spirit, and humbly obedient to the Father (Luke 1:31-35; 2:52; 4:1; Heb 10:5).

Luke 1:35
And the angel answered her, "The Holy Spirit will come upon you, and the power of the Most High will overshadow you; therefore the child to be born will be called holy—the Son of God.

72 What was God's design for the incarnation?

Christ endured the humiliation and weakness of humanity and **willingly died in our place to purchase our redemption and give glory to God** (John 10:17-18; Phil 2:5-11).

John 10:17
For this reason the Father loves me, because I lay down my life that I may take it up again.

73 Why do we call God the Son, Jesus Christ?

God commanded Joseph and Mary to call him *Jesus*, which **means "God saves."** *Christ* **is a title meaning** "anointed one," or **"Messiah"** (Matt 1:21; John 4:25; Isa 61:1-2).

John 4:25
The woman said to him, "I know that Messiah is coming (he who is called Christ). When he comes, he will tell us all things."

74 What three offices does Jesus fulfill?

Both in his incarnation and exaltation, **Jesus perfectly fulfills the three Old Testament offices of Prophet, Priest, and King** (Acts 3:22; Heb 5:6; Ps 2:6).

Acts 3:22
Moses said, 'The Lord God will raise up for you a prophet like me from your brothers. You shall listen to him in whatever he tells you.

75 How is Jesus the perfect Prophet?

He reveals God, fulfills all the prophecies about the Messiah, **and teaches us God's will. Without him we would be ignorant** of God and his saving love (John 1:18; 1 Pet 1:10-12; 2 Cor 4:3-6).

John 1:18
No one has ever seen God; the only God, who is at the Father's side, he has made him known.

76 How is Jesus the perfect Priest?

He offered himself as a perfect sacrifice, reconciles us to God, **and continually mediates between us and God. Without him we would remain guilty** of sin and separated from God (Heb 2:17; 9:24; 1 Tim 2:5-6).

Hebrews 9:24
For Christ has entered, not into holy places made with hands, which are copies of the true things, but into heaven itself, now to appear in the presence of God on our behalf.

77 How is Jesus the perfect King?

He rules over all creation and accomplishes his perfect plans, **guiding and protecting the redeemed. Without him we would be helpless** and left to follow our shifting passions (Rom 8:28; Eph 1:19-21; Rev 1:5-6; Rom 1:24-26).

Revelation 1:5–6
...Jesus Christ the faithful witness, the firstborn of the dead, and the ruler of kings on earth. To him who loves us and has freed us from our sins by his blood and made us a kingdom, priests to his God and Father, to him be glory and dominion forever and ever.

78 Why was Jesus' life and sacrifice effective for salvation?

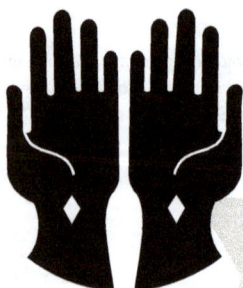

Because God made him who knew no sin to be counted as sin for us, and then credited us with his righteousness. His death fully satisfied God's just wrath and thereby delivers us from the power and penalty of sin. **This is called "penal substitutionary atonement"** (2 Cor 5:21; Col 1:21-22).

2 Corinthians 5:21
For our sake he made him to be sin who knew no sin, so that in him we might become the righteousness of God.

79 What else does Christ's death redeem?

Christ's death is the first fruits of the redemption and renewal of **every part of fallen creation.** The whole creation groans in eager anticipation of the final glory of Christ's perfect reign (Col 1:19-20; Rom 8:20-23).

Colossians 1:19–20
For in him all the fullness of God was pleased to dwell, and through him to reconcile to himself all things, whether on earth or in heaven, making peace by the blood of his cross.

80 Is the death of Christ sufficient to cover the sins of all people?

Yes. The death of Christ is sufficient to cover every sin ever committed, **but is only effective for the elect** (John 3:16; 1 John 2:2-3; John 10:11; Eph 1:4-7).

John 10:11
I am the good shepherd. The good shepherd lays down his life for the sheep.

81 Did Jesus stay dead?

No. On the third day, Jesus rose bodily from the grave, according to the Scriptures, and was seen by eyewitnesses, including over five hundred at once. **He ascended into heaven and promised to return again** to judge the living and the dead (1 Cor 15:4-6; Acts 1:9-11; 2 Tim 4:1).

1 Corinthians 15:4–6
that he was buried, that he was raised on the third day in accordance with the Scriptures, and that he appeared to Cephas, then to the twelve. Then he appeared to more than five hundred brothers at one time, most of whom are still alive, though some have fallen asleep.

GOD THE HOLY SPIRIT

82 Who did Jesus promise to send to the redeemed?

God the Holy Spirit permanently dwells within us, comforts us, and intercedes for us, even when we don't know how to pray. His ministry in this age began at Pentecost, when he came from the Father sent by the Son (Rom 8:9, 26-27; John 14:15-17; Acts 2:33).

John 14:16-17
And I will ask the Father, and he will give you another Helper, to be with you forever, even the Spirit of truth, whom the world cannot receive, because it neither sees him nor knows him. You know him, for he dwells with you and will be in you.

83 Did the Holy Spirit also dwell in Jesus Christ?

Yes. The Holy Spirit was given to Jesus without measure, and he perfectly depended upon the Spirit to live a holy life, perform miracles, and receive God's strength (Luke 4:1; John 3:34; Mark 3:28-30).

Luke 4:1
And Jesus, full of the Holy Spirit, returned from the Jordan and was led by the Spirit in the wilderness

84 What do we believe about the Holy Spirit?

That he is God, coeternal with the Father and the Son. He is a distinct person, yet equal in nature, power, and glory, and should be worshiped with the Father and the Son (Gen 1:2; Acts 5:3-4).

Genesis 1:2
The earth was without form and void, and darkness was over the face of the deep. And the Spirit of God was hovering over the face of the waters.

85 What role does the Holy Spirit play in securing our Redemption?

The Holy Spirit regenerates our hearts, draws us to Christ, **convicts us of sin**, grants us faith to believe, **and unites us to Christ** (Ezek 36:26; Eph 1:13-14; 2:8; 1 Cor 12:13).

Ezekiel 36:26
And I will give you a new heart, and a new spirit I will put within you. And I will remove the heart of stone from your flesh and give you a heart of flesh.

86 How does the Holy Spirit continue to help us?

The Holy Spirit assures us of our salvation, guides us, sanctifies us, enables us to pray, **and helps us understand God's Word** (Rom 8:9, 12-17, 26-30; 1 Cor 2:12-13; 2 Cor 3:18).

Romans 8:16
The Spirit himself bears witness with our spirit that we are children of God,

87 What is the fruit of the Holy Spirit?

The fruit of the Spirit is love, joy, peace, patience, kindness, goodness, faithfulness, gentleness, and self-control. The redeemed will walk in the ways of the Spirit, gradually growing in righteousness and exhibiting this fruit (Gal 5:22-25; Eph 5:18-20).

Galatians 5:24–25
And those who belong to Christ Jesus have crucified the flesh with its passions and desires. If we live by the Spirit, let us also keep in step with the Spirit.

88   What are spiritual gifts?

Spiritual gifts are specific abilities given to the redeemed for the purpose of building up the church, spreading the gospel, and ministering to one another (1 Cor 12:7; 14:12; Eph 4:11-13; Rom 12:4-8).

1 Corinthians 14:12
12So with yourselves, since you are eager for manifestations of the Spirit, strive to excel in building up the church.

89   Are the miraculous gifts still in operation in the church today?

Cessationism: **No. The miraculous gifts**, such as the speaking in tongues, prophetic revelation, and healing, **ceased with the end of the apostolic age.** In the New Testament, these gifts are associated with the ministry of the apostles, **and there is little to no evidence of the continuation of these gifts in** most of **church history.** However, even though the miraculous gifts have ceased to operate normatively in the church, God is able to perform miracles whenever he so desires (2 Cor 12:12; Heb 2:3-4; Eph 2:20; 1 Cor 13:8-10).

✷ *Continuationism:* **Yes. The miraculous gifts,** such as the speaking in tongues, prophetic revelation, and healing, **continue in the church today. Since the giving of the gifts is tied to the mission of the church, the gifts will cease only when Christ returns.** Historical evidence, especially in the 20th century, points to the continuation of the gifts for the church today. However, the practice of the miraculous sign-gifts must always be for the building up of the church, and carefully administered by church leaders (1 Cor 13:8-10; 14:13-19).

1 Corinthians 13:8–10
Love never ends. As for prophecies, they will pass away; as for tongues, they will cease; as for knowledge, it will pass away. For we know in part and we prophesy in part, but when the perfect comes, the partial will pass away.

SALVATION

ELECTION AND CALLING

90 Is salvation first a work of God or a free choice of man?

Salvation is first a work of God, entirely a work of grace, "even as he chose us in Christ before the foundation of the world, that we should be holy and blameless before him." (Eph 1:4; Rom 9:15-16).

Romans 9:15–16
For he says to Moses, "I will have mercy on whom I have mercy, and I will have compassion on whom I have compassion." So then it depends not on human will or exertion, but on God, who has mercy.

91 Is there any grace that God shows commonly to all humanity?

Yes. In God's common grace to all humanity, **he reveals himself, restrains evil**, gives governments, sustains societal structures, **and provides for our daily needs** (Ps 145:9; Rom 1:19; 2:14-15; 13:1-7; Gen 4:20-22; Matt 5:45).

Psalm 145:9
The LORD is good to all, and his mercy is over all that he has made.

92 Are all people saved who experience God's common grace?

No. Only those elected and effectively called by God are saved. The rest are hardened and left in sin and death. Even so, God desires all men to come to a saving knowledge of him (Acts 13:48; Rom 11:7-8; 1 Tim 2:4).

Acts 13:48
And when the Gentiles heard this, they began rejoicing and glorifying the word of the Lord, and as many as were appointed to eternal life believed.

93 What is God's effective call?

God's call always begins with the preaching of the gospel which becomes effective as **a work of the Holy Spirit that** regenerates our hearts, **convicts us of our sin, enlightens our minds** to know and cherish Christ, **and draws us to respond in repentance and faith** (John 6:44; Rom 8:29).

John 6:44
No one can come to me unless the Father who sent me draws him. And I will raise him up on the last day.

94 Does the preaching of the gospel always produce gospel fruit?

No. The very same preaching of the gospel will prove effective for some and folly for others, based on God's electing grace (Isa 6:8-12; Rom 10:14-15; 2 Cor 2:15-16).

2 Corinthians 2:15–16

For we are the aroma of Christ to God among those who are being saved and among those who are perishing, to one a fragrance from death to death, to the other a fragrance from life to life. Who is sufficient for these things?

REGENERATION

95   What is regeneration?

Regeneration is the work of the Holy Spirit by which he removes our dead heart and gives us a living heart. Thus, we are born again. The Holy Spirit, at the moment of regeneration, permanently indwells every believer, uniting them to Christ (Titus 3:5; John 3:5-8; Ezek 36:26-27; Rom 8:9; Eph 1:13).

Titus 3:5
he saved us, not because of works done by us in righteousness, but according to his own mercy, by the washing of regeneration and renewal of the Holy Spirit,

96   Does hearing the Word of God always precede regeneration?

Yes. The Word of God is the means by which the Holy Spirit regenerates sinful people. The Holy Spirit makes the reading, and especially the preaching of the Word, an effective means of converting, convincing, and comforting (Ps 19:8; Rom 1:15-16; 2 Tim 3:15).

Romans 1:16
For I am not ashamed of the gospel, for it is the power of God for salvation to everyone who believes, to the Jew first and also to the Greek.

97 Does faith come before regeneration?

No. It is only the new heart, moved by the Spirit, **that can respond in repentance and faith** (John 3:8; 2 Cor 5:17).

John 3:8
The wind blows where it wishes, and you hear its sound, but you do not know where it comes from or where it goes. So it is with everyone who is born of the Spirit."

98 What is the proof of regeneration?

The proof of regeneration is **a repentant faith, which results in a whole life devoted to turning from sin and giving glory to God** in all that we do (Ezek 11:19-20; Col 3:17).

Colossians 3:17
And whatever you do, in word or deed, do everything in the name of the Lord Jesus, giving thanks to God the Father through him.

99 How does God baptize and seal us by the Spirit?

In connection with the work of the Spirit in regeneration, **Christ baptizes us by the Spirit into his body and the Father seals us with the Spirit so that we belong to God.** Therefore, we are permanently declared righteous and adopted into his eternal family (Eph 1:13-14; 1 Cor 12:12-13; 2 Cor 1:21-22).

1 Corinthians 12:12–13
For just as the body is one and has many members, and all the members of the body, though many, are one body, so it is with Christ. For in one Spirit we were all baptized into one body—Jews or Greeks, slaves or free—and all were made to drink of one Spirit.

CONVERSION

100 What is a summary of the gospel message?

Four main ideas summarize the gospel message that we all must know and believe to be converted. **First, God is the one true**, holy, and Triune **God, who requires perfect obedience to his law** for our good and as an expression of his love. **Second, every person has fallen short of this law and deserves** eternal punishment in **hell. Third, God sent his Son to** live the perfect life we could not live, **die on the cross in our place, and rise again on the third day**, thereby paying the penalty for all our sin. **Fourth, in response, we must repent of sin and believe this gospel** (Rom 1:19-20, 24-26; 3:23; 5:8; 10:9).

Romans 5:8
but God shows his love for us in that while we were still sinners, Christ died for us.

101 What is repentance?

Repentance is recognizing sin as sin, grieving and hating it, then **turning from sin, dying to self**, renewing the mind, **and following Christ** and all his ways (Luke 9:23; Eph 4:22-24).

Luke 9:23
And he said to all, "If anyone would come after me, let him deny himself and take up his cross daily and follow me."

102 What does it mean to die to self and follow Christ?

We must aim to avoid all sin and idolatry and live for the glory of God; to **seek true joy in Christ rather than in what we think will make us happy** (Gal 2:20; Rom 12:1-2; 14:17).

Galatians 2:20
I have been crucified with Christ. It is no longer I who live, but Christ who lives in me. And the life I now live in the flesh I live by faith in the Son of God, who loved me and gave himself for me.

103 What is saving faith?

Saving faith knows and **affirms** gospel truth revealed in God's Word **and trusts in the person and work of Christ**, resting on him alone for salvation (Heb 11:1, 8; Rom 6:8-9; 10:9; Phil 3:8-9).

Romans 10:9
...if you confess with your mouth that Jesus is Lord and believe in your heart that God raised him from the dead, you will be saved.

104 Can we separate repentance and saving faith?

No. Repentance and faith are inseparable experiences of God's grace, **because saving faith is always a repentant faith.** We cannot truly believe without turning from sin, and we cannot truly turn from sin without believing (Mark 1:15; Luke 9:23).

Mark 1:15
and saying, "The time is fulfilled, and the kingdom of God is at hand; repent and believe in the gospel."

105 Since salvation is by God's grace alone, is our faith also a gift?

Yes. "For by grace you are saved through faith, and this is not from yourselves; it is God's gift." Like regeneration, repentant faith is a gift from the Holy Spirit (Eph 2:8 CSB; Titus 3:4-6; 2 Tim 2:25).

2 Timothy 2:25b
...God may perhaps grant them repentance leading to a knowledge of the truth,

106 Can we purposefully pursue a sinful lifestyle and expect to be saved?

No. A repentant faith always hates sin and seeks to live for Christ and die to self (2 Cor 5:15; 1 John 3:5-6).

1 John 3:5–6
You know that he appeared in order to take away sins, and in him there is no sin. No one who abides in him keeps on sinning; no one who keeps on sinning has either seen him or known him.

107 Does conversion happen in a moment or slowly over time?

Conversion happens in a moment, when the Father draws us to the Son by the regenerating work of the Spirit as we repent and believe for the first time. However, God may prepare our hearts over time and thus we might not know the precise moment of conversion, only that our repentant faith is genuine (John 6:44; Acts 2:38; 1 John 5:1).

1 John 5:1
Everyone who believes that Jesus is the Christ has been born of God, and everyone who loves the Father loves whoever has been born of him.

108 What is the summary of our faith presented in the Apostles' Creed?

We believe in God the Father Almighty, Maker of heaven and earth; and in Jesus Christ his only Son our Lord, who was conceived by the Holy Spirit, born of the virgin Mary, suffered under Pontius Pilate, was crucified, died, and was buried. He descended into the realm of the dead. The third day he rose again from the dead. He ascended into heaven and is seated at the right hand of God the Father Almighty; from there he will come to judge the living and the dead. We believe in the Holy Spirit, the holy and universal church, the communion of saints, the forgiveness of sins, the resurrection of the body, and the life everlasting (Jude 3).

JUSTIFICATION AND SANCTIFICATION

109 What is the difference between justification and sanctification?

Justification is our declared righteousness before God, our settled standing at the point of conversion. **Sanctification is our gradual growing in righteousness** that continues until our death or the Lord's return (Rom 5:8-9; 6:22; Heb 10:14).

Hebrews 10:14
For by a single offering he has perfected for all time those who are being sanctified.

110 How is it that we are justified before God?

By grace, God proclaims our sins forgiven and credits Christ's righteousness to us. This happens the moment we repent and believe through our union with Christ (Rom 3:24-26; 2 Cor 5:19-21).

Romans 3:24-25
and are justified by his grace as a gift, through the redemption that is in Christ Jesus, whom God put forward as a propitiation by his blood, to be received by faith. This was to show God's righteousness, because in his divine forbearance he had passed over former sins.

111 What are the benefits of our union with Christ?

Because we are one with Christ, we are a new creation united with him in his death and resurrection; all the blessings of salvation are ours in Christ and we are united with one another in Christ's body, the church (John 17:20-23; Eph 1:3; Gal 3:28).

Ephesians 1:3
Blessed be the God and Father of our Lord Jesus Christ, who has blessed us in Christ with every spiritual blessing in the heavenly places,

112 What are the benefits of God's adoption?

In spite of our sinful rebellion, **we have the full rights and privileges of children of God, fellow heirs with Jesus Christ.** Therefore, our inheritance is eternal, imperishable, and exceedingly valuable (Rom 8:16-17; 1 Pet 1:3-4; Eph 1:5-6).

1 Peter 1:3–4
Blessed be the God and Father of our Lord Jesus Christ! According to his great mercy, he has caused us to be born again to a living hope through the resurrection of Jesus Christ from the dead, to an inheritance that is imperishable, undefiled, and unfading, kept in heaven for you,

113 Should we seek to be justified through good works?

No. Everything necessary to salvation is found in Christ alone. To attempt to earn God's favor through good works is to deny the sufficiency of Christ's work of redemption (Gal 2:16, 21; Eph 2:8-9).

Galatians 2:21
I do not nullify the grace of God, for if righteousness were through the law, then Christ died for no purpose.

114 Are good works a necessary part of the Christian life?

Yes. Christ not only justifies us but sanctifies us. He created us "for good works, which God prepared beforehand, that we should walk in them." Considering all the benefits that are ours in Christ, our lives ought to show love and gratitude to him (Eph 2:10; Rom 12:1-2).

Romans 12:1
I appeal to you therefore, brothers, by the mercies of God, to present your bodies as a living sacrifice, holy and acceptable to God, which is your spiritual worship.

115 What is the best evidence that our salvation is genuine?

1 John gives us three evidences of genuine salvation: a repentant faith, a consistent obedience, and a love for other Christians. James says, "Faith without works is dead," and so we see that the best evidence of our salvation is **sanctification. Every genuine Christian will grow in holiness and produce fruit** (1 John 5:1-5; Jas 2:17; 1 Thess 4:3; Luke 8:15).

1 Thessalonians 4:3
For this is the will of God, your sanctification: that you abstain from sexual immorality;

116 How does God use sanctification to bless us in this life?

As the Holy Spirit sanctifies, **he protects us from the damaging effects of sin**, comforts us when we are discouraged, **and helps us live for God's glory** (Prov 4:18; 1 Cor 10:13, 31; 2 Cor 1:3-4).

Proverbs 4:18
But the path of the righteous is like the light of dawn, which shines brighter and brighter until full day.

117 How secure is our salvation?

Completely secure, for our assurance rests on the faithful nature of God and the finished work of Christ. For God says, "nothing… can separate us from the love of God in Christ Jesus our Lord" (Rom 8:38-39; John 10:28-29).

John 10:28–29
I give them eternal life, and they will never perish, and no one will snatch them out of my hand. My Father, who has given them to me, is greater than all, and no one is able to snatch them out of the Father's hand.

118 How do we know that our faith will persevere to the end?

God promises that "he who began a good work in you will bring it to completion at the day of Jesus Christ." (Phil 1:6; Heb 13:5; 1 Pet 1:5)

Hebrews 13:5
Keep your life free from love of money, and be content with what you have, for he has said, "I will never leave you nor forsake you."

119 What is the final hope of our salvation?

To partake in the blessed resurrection, when we will **be given a glorified body and dwell in the presence of God forever**, free from sin in the new heavens and the new earth (John 3:16; Rom 5:2; 8:30; Rev 20:6).

Romans 8:30
And those whom he predestined he also called, and those whom he called he also justified, and those whom he justified he also glorified.

CHURCH

THE LOCAL CHURCH

120 What is a church?

A church is a Spirit-regenerated, new covenant **community of individuals united to Christ by faith**, committed to one another, and Biblically **organized into one local body. Baptism** as a believer **inaugurates** membership into that body, **and the Lord's Supper signifies our ongoing union** (Heb 12:22-24; Jer 31:33-34; Lu 22:20; 1 Cor 12:12-13, 10:17).

1 Corinthians 10:17
Because there is one bread, we who are many are one body, for we all partake of the one bread.

121 How does the universal church relate to the local church?

The universal church includes every Spirit-regenerated, new covenant **believer** from the inception of the church until Christ returns. **Local churches are gatherings of the universal church** (Eph 1:22-23; 2 Thess 1:1).

Ephesians 1:22-23
And he put all things under his feet and gave him as head over all things to the church, which is his body, the fullness of him who fills all in all.

122 When did the church begin?

At the day of Pentecost, when the Holy Spirit came in power regenerating three-thousand souls through the preaching of Peter. Before that point, the Holy Spirit did not permanently indwell anyone, nor did the disciples come together regularly to worship Christ. **On the same day the universal church began, a local church was formed in Jerusalem** (Acts 2:37-47).

Acts 2:41
So those who received his word were baptized, and there were added that day about three thousand souls.

123 Can we belong to the universal church but not a local church?

It is possible to be regenerated and yet unable to join a local church; **however, this is extremely rare. The normal Christian life is in constant connection to a local church** as an integrated member of the body of Christ (Rom 12:4-8; Heb 10:24-25).

Hebrews 10:24–25
And let us consider how to stir up one another to love and good works, not neglecting to meet together, as is the habit of some, but encouraging one another, and all the more as you see the Day drawing near.

124 What does a local church do?

A local church gathers regularly to worship **around the preaching and reading of the Word of God**, the celebration of the ordinances, the edification of one another, and the pursuit of holiness. **A church scatters to evangelize the lost**, engages in acts of mercy, and in all ways aims to glorify God (1 Tim 4:13; Matt 28:19-20).

1 Timothy 4:13
Until I come, devote yourself to the public reading of Scripture, to exhortation, to teaching.

125 Must a church gather only on Sundays?

No. It is not commanded in the Bible, **but historically Christians regularly met on Sundays** for corporate worship, **calling this first day of the week "the Lord's Day," to celebrate Christ's resurrection.** Therefore, it is common and prudent for churches to continue this tradition (Acts 20:7; 1 Cor 16:2; Rev 1:10).

1 Corinthians 16:2
On the first day of every week, each of you is to put something aside and store it up, as he may prosper, so that there will be no collecting when I come.

126 Should Sabbath regulations apply to the Lord's Day?

No. We are free in Christ to enjoy a variety of activities on Sunday, so long as we do not forsake corporate worship and aim to enjoy regular periods of rest from our normal activities (Mark 2:27-28; Gal 4:9-10; Heb 10:25; Gen 2:2-3).

Mark 2:27–28
And he said to them, "The Sabbath was made for man, not man for the Sabbath. So the Son of Man is lord even of the Sabbath."

127 What is the primary goal of the preaching ministry of the church?

To preach the Word, making the main point of the text the main point of the sermon, and applying it to the Christian life. Although the gospel should be evident in all sermons, preaching is not primarily for the unbeliever, but for the building up of the redeemed (2 Tim 4:2-4; Neh 8:8).

2 Timothy 4:2
preach the word; be ready in season and out of season; reprove, rebuke, and exhort, with complete patience and teaching.

128 Should churches ever separate from other churches or Christian organizations?

Yes. Churches should only cooperate for the sake of gospel ministry with other churches and organizations **that clearly hold to the gospel message.** However, since cooperation and interdependence are important biblical values, separation is always a tragic consequence of apostasy or heresy (2 Tim 3:1-5; 2 John 7-11).

2 John 9–11
Everyone who goes on ahead and does not abide in the teaching of Christ, does not have God. Whoever abides in the teaching has both the Father and the Son. If anyone comes to you and does not bring this teaching, do not receive him into your house or give him any greeting, for whoever greets him takes part in his wicked works.

129 Should local churches be self-governed?

Yes. Each local church should be autonomous—free from external authority or control. However, churches can and should cooperate with other churches and organizations to further the impact of gospel ministry (Titus 1:5; Phil 4:14-18).

Titus 1:5
This is why I left you in Crete, so that you might put what remained into order, and appoint elders in every town as I directed you—

130 What leaders did Christ give to the church?

He first gave Apostles through whom we received the New Testament. **Today, he gives the church two offices: pastor-elders and deacons. All church members** are called to recognize and affirm their leaders as well as **guard the purity of the gospel** message and gospel witness **through church discipline** (Eph 4:11-12; 1 Tim 3:1, 13; Heb 13:7, 17; 1 Cor 5:4-5).

Hebrews 13:7
Remember your leaders, those who spoke to you the word of God. Consider the outcome of their way of life, and imitate their faith.

131 Who can become pastor-elders?

Biblically qualified men proven to be above reproach, and **capable of teaching**, leading, shepherding, **and protecting the doctrine of the church** in the love of Christ (1 Tim 3:1-7; 1 Pet 5:1-3).

1 Timothy 3:1–2a
The saying is trustworthy: If anyone aspires to the office of overseer, he desires a noble task. Therefore an overseer must be above reproach,

132 Who can become deacons?

Biblically qualified men and women proven to be above reproach, and **capable of organizing ministry**, administrating, serving, **and protecting the unity of the church** in the love of Christ (1 Tim 3:8-13, Acts 6:1-7).

1 Timothy 3:8–10
Deacons likewise must be dignified, not double-tongued, not addicted to much wine, not greedy for dishonest gain. They must hold the mystery of the faith with a clear conscience. And let them also be tested first; then let them serve as deacons if they prove themselves blameless.

133 Is church membership biblical?

Yes. In the book of Acts the early church kept rolls, lists, and numbers of those who joined the church. Further, church leaders are called to watch over their flock, and individuals are called to submit to leaders and guard one another, which is only possible in the context of clearly defined church membership (Acts 2:41, 47; 1 Tim 5:9; Heb 12:14-15; 13:17; 1 Cor 12:27).

Acts 2:47b
And the Lord added to their number day by day those who were being saved.

134   What is church discipline?

Church discipline is a process of accountability for our good, laid out by Christ in Matthew 18. If church members continue in sin, they are lovingly confronted: first, by individuals; second, by two or three; **and** third, by the whole church. If they refuse to listen to the church, they are to be removed from membership. Discipline **always has the goal of restoration** and results in protecting the purity and witness of the church (Matt 18:15-20; 1 Cor 5).

Matthew 18:15
If your brother sins against you, go and tell him his fault, between you and him alone. If he listens to you, you have gained your brother.

135   What are the consequences of church discipline?

If professing Christians remain in sin following the discipline process, they are, by the same church, kept from the ordinance of the Lord's Supper and removed from membership. As far as we can tell, unless they are restored, they remain in apostasy and will not inherit the kingdom of heaven (Matt 18:17-18; 1 Cor 5:4-5; 11).

1 Corinthians 5:4–5
When you are assembled in the name of the Lord Jesus and my spirit is present, with the power of our Lord Jesus, you are to deliver this man to Satan for the destruction of the flesh, so that his spirit may be saved in the day of the Lord.

136 What are the keys of the kingdom of heaven?

The affirmation of the gospel message and church discipline, by which heaven is opened to the regenerate and shut for the unbeliever. The keys are held by the entire membership of the church who affirm the gospel and exercise church discipline (Matt 16:19; 18:18).

Matthew 18:18
Truly, I say to you, whatever you bind on earth shall be bound in heaven, and whatever you loose on earth shall be loosed in heaven.

ORDINANCES

137 How many ordinances did God give the church, and why?

There are **two** ordinances: **Baptism and the Lord's Supper.** They are given by God, instituted by Christ, rendered effective by the Holy Spirit, and clear symbols of gospel truth. **As visible signs reflecting God's saving work, they unite Christians together as a local body in gospel harmony.** Just as we are one with Christ in his death, burial, and resurrection, we are one with one another (Acts 2:38, 41; Luke 22:19-20).

Luke 22:19–20
And he took bread, and when he had given thanks, he broke it and gave it to them, saying, "This is my body, which is given for you. Do this in remembrance of me." And likewise the cup after they had eaten, saying, "This cup that is poured out for you is the new covenant in my blood."

138 What is baptism?

Baptism is a church's act of affirming and portraying a believer's union with Christ by immersion in the name of the Father, Son, and Holy Spirit; **and a believer's act of publicly committing to Christ and his church,** thereby distinguishing them from the world (Rom 6:3-5; Matt 28:19).

Romans 6:4
We were buried therefore with him by baptism into death, in order that, just as Christ was raised from the dead by the glory of the Father, we too might walk in newness of life.

139   Does baptism with water wash away sin?

No. Baptism only represents regeneration like a picture; the washing of water representing the purifying work of the blood of Christ to cleanse us from all sin (1 John 1:7; 1 Pet 3:18, 21).

1 John 1:7
But if we walk in the light, as he is in the light, we have fellowship with one another, and the blood of Jesus his Son cleanses us from all sin.

140   Who should be baptized?

Every regenerated **believer in Christ should be baptized** because Christ commanded us to declare our faith through this ordinance. However, since baptism inaugurates church membership, only those prepared to join the church should be baptized (Matt 28:19; Acts 2:38; 10:48).

Acts 10:48
And he commanded them to be baptized in the name of Jesus Christ. Then they asked him to remain for some days.

141 Should infants of Christian families ever be baptized?

No. Infants are unable to confess the gospel message, thus they cannot be members of the church like their parents (Luke 3:7-8; Acts 18:8).

Acts 18:8
Crispus, the ruler of the synagogue, believed in the Lord, together with his entire household. And many of the Corinthians hearing Paul believed and were baptized.

142 How can we determine if our baptism is valid?

If our baptism occurred after our conversion, and if it was associated with the preaching of the true gospel (Acts 8:12; Rom 6:4).

Acts 8:12
But when they believed Philip as he preached good news about the kingdom of God and the name of Jesus Christ, they were baptized, both men and women.

143 What is the Lord's Supper or Communion?

The Lord's Supper is a church's act of celebrating our union with Christ as the many commune together in one body; **and a believer's act of partaking the bread and cup.** In this Supper we remember Christ's death—his body and blood, broken and shed, as a perfect substitute for every sin— and anticipate his return (1 Cor 10:16-17; 11:23-26).

1 Corinthians 10:16–17
The cup of blessing that we bless, is it not a participation in the blood of Christ? The bread that we break, is it not a participation in the body of Christ? Because there is one bread, we who are many are one body, for we all partake of the one bread.

144 Does the Lord's Supper add anything to Christ's atoning work?

No. Christ died once for all our sins. The Lord's Supper celebrates and remembers Christ's atoning work as a picture that encourages us to look to all that he has done for us (Rom 4:24-25; Heb 9:25-28; Matt 26:26-28).

Romans 4:24–25
It will be counted to us who believe in him who raised from the dead Jesus our Lord, who was delivered up for our trespasses and raised for our justification.

145 Who should partake of the Lord's Supper?

Only baptized believers who do not possess a divisive and unrepentant spirit and who remain in good standing with their local church. Those who take the Lord's Supper in an unworthy manner eat and drink judgment to themselves (Matt 5:23-24; 1 Cor 12:13; 11:27-30).

1 Corinthians 12:13
For in one Spirit we were all baptized into one body—Jews or Greeks, slaves or free— and all were made to drink of one Spirit.

146 How should we prepare to take the Lord's Supper?

With these five looks: (one) look up to thank God for the gift of Christ, (two) look within in repentant self-examination, (three) look back at the work of Christ on the cross, (four) look ahead to Christ's return, and (five) look around to celebrate our union with one another, just as we are one with Christ (1 Cor 11:26-33).

1 Corinthians 11:26
For as often as you eat this bread and drink the cup, you proclaim the Lord's death until he comes.

147 Where and when should we take the Lord's Supper?

When a church gathers corporately, we take the Lord's Supper as a symbol of union with one another and with Christ (Acts 20:7; 1 Cor 10:16-17; 11:33).

Acts 20:7
On the first day of the week, when we were gathered together to break bread, Paul talked with them, intending to depart on the next day, and he prolonged his speech until midnight.

148 Should we take communion at non-gospel preaching churches?

No. In those settings there is no true union with Christ to celebrate (1 Cor 5:6-11; 2 Cor 6:15).

2 Corinthians 6:15
What accord has Christ with Belial? Or what portion does a believer share with an unbeliever?

THE
CHRISTIAN
LIFE

PRAYER

149 What is prayer?

Prayer is pouring out the desires of our hearts to God. We pray to the Father, in the name of the Son, by the power of the Holy Spirit, for things agreeable to God's will, trusting him to guide and answer (Ps 62:8; John 16:23; 1 John 5:14).

Psalm 62:8
Trust in him at all times, O people; pour out your heart before him; God is a refuge for us.

150 What are the five main types of prayer?

Praise, confession of sin, petition, thanksgiving, and lament (Pss 150; 51:1-12; 1 Tim 2:1; Ps 13).

1 Timothy 2:1
First of all, then, I urge that supplications, prayers, intercessions, and thanksgivings be made for all people,

151   Why is prayer necessary?

We must pray to commune with God; recognizing him alone as God, expressing our dependence, and **orienting our hearts towards him at every moment** (Phil 4:6; 1 Thess 5:16-18).

1 Thessalonians 5:16–18
Rejoice always, pray without ceasing, give thanks in all circumstances; for this is the will of God in Christ Jesus for you.

152   What should we pray?

The whole Word of God directs us in what we should pray as we learn to take words that originated in the heart and mind of God and circulate them through our hearts and minds back to God (Eph 3:14-16; John 6:63).

John 6:63
It is the Spirit who gives life; the flesh is no help at all. The words that I have spoken to you are spirit and life.

153 How can we learn to pray?

One example to consider: **read the Bible, stop after each verse, meditate, and pray.** In particular, Jesus teaches us to pray by giving us the Lord's Prayer (Pss 1:2; 119:9-16).

Psalm 119:13–16
With my lips I declare all the rules of your mouth. In the way of your testimonies I delight as much as in all riches. I will meditate on your precepts and fix my eyes on your ways. I will delight in your statutes; I will not forget your word.

154 What is the Lord's Prayer?

"Our Father in heaven, hallowed be your name. Your kingdom come, your will be done, on earth as it is in heaven. Give us this day our daily bread, and forgive us our debts as we also have forgiven our debtors. And lead us not into temptation, but deliver us from evil. For yours is the kingdom and the power and the glory, forever. Amen." (Matt 6:9-13)

155 Must we always use this form of prayer?

No. Each phrase can act as a topic that guides and directs our prayers as we pour out the desires of our hearts to God (Matt 6:7-8).

Matthew 6:7
And when you pray, do not heap up empty phrases as the Gentiles do, for they think that they will be heard for their many words.

SCRIPTURE READING

156 How is the Word of God to be read and heard?

With diligence, preparation, and prayer, relying upon the Holy Spirit to illumine God's words to our minds and help us apply his truth to our lives (Ps 119:18; 2 Tim 2:15; Eph 1:17-18).

Psalm 119:18
Open my eyes, that I may behold wondrous things out of your law.

157 What are five ways to approach the Bible?

We should: (one) read the Bible, **(two) listen** to the Bible read and taught, **(three) study** the Bible diligently, **(four) memorize** key verses, **and (five) meditate regularly on God's words.** As we know it is good to eat a balanced diet, so too are we to have a balanced approach to the Word of God (Acts 17:11; Pss 1:2-3; 40:8).

Psalm 40:8
I delight to do your will, O my God; your law is within my heart.

EVANGELISM

158 Has God commanded us to proclaim the gospel to all people?

Yes. God commands his people to proclaim the gospel to everyone, even unto the ends of the earth, **so that some will be saved.** Sharing the gospel with unbelievers is something we can do in this life that we cannot do in the next (Matt 28:19; Rom 10:13-15; 1 Tim 2:1-4).

Romans 10:14–15
How then will they call on him in whom they have not believed? And how are they to believe in him of whom they have never heard? And how are they to hear without someone preaching? And how are they to preach unless they are sent? As it is written, "How beautiful are the feet of those who preach the good news!"

159 How should we feel about those who have not trusted in Jesus?

Our hearts should mourn and grow with compassion towards all unbelievers, and thus be motivated to share the gospel (Rom 9:1-3; Jonah 4:1-4, 10-11).

Romans 9:2–3
I have great sorrow and unceasing anguish in my heart. For I could wish that I myself were accursed and cut off from Christ for the sake of my brothers, my kinsmen according to the flesh.

160 How are we to do the work of evangelism?

By showing our Redeemer through our redeemed life, praying for the effective movement of the Holy Spirit, **and compassionately using God's Word to communicate God's gospel** (Col 4:3-6; Heb 4:12).

Colossians 4:5–6
Walk in wisdom toward outsiders, making the best use of the time. Let your speech always be gracious, seasoned with salt, so that you may know how you ought to answer each person.

161 What is the goal of evangelism?

To explain the gospel clearly and trust the Holy Spirit to regenerate hearts in order to **make lifelong disciples of Jesus Christ.** Then we aim to gather those disciples into self-sustaining churches (Acts 4:12, 29; Col 1:28-29; Acts 2:47).

Acts 4:12
And there is salvation in no one else, for there is no other name under heaven given among men by which we must be saved.

162 What is the relationship between evangelism and missions?

Missions includes evangelism that leads to establish and strengthen local churches in a geographic, linguistic, or cultural setting different than our own. Missions work is necessary to fulfill Christ's Great Commission (Matt 28:19-20; Acts 14:21-26).

Acts 14:21–23
When they had preached the gospel to that city and had made many disciples, they returned to Lystra and to Iconium and to Antioch, strengthening the souls of the disciples, encouraging them to continue in the faith, and saying that through many tribulations we must enter the kingdom of God. And when they had appointed elders for them in every church, with prayer and fasting they committed them to the Lord in whom they had believed.

DISCIPLESHIP

163 What is discipleship?

Intentionally investing your life into others with the goal of growing together in Christian knowledge, affections, and applications, **so that you can present each other mature in Christ** (Titus 2:1-8; Col 1:28-29).

Colossians 1:28–29
Him we proclaim, warning everyone and teaching everyone with all wisdom, that we may present everyone mature in Christ. For this I toil, struggling with all his energy that he powerfully works within me.

164 Is discipleship for all Christians?

Yes. The New Testament frequently commands every Christian to love and care for one another, faithfully helping one another to live holy lives (1 John 4:7-8; Heb 10:24; Eph 4:25).

1 John 4:7
Beloved, let us love one another, for love is from God, and whoever loves has been born of God and knows God.

165 How is discipleship done?

By regularly spending time with other Christians, **engaging in purposeful conversations** that teach and correct, doing ministry together, **and modeling Christlikeness** (Acts 20:18-20; Deut 6:4-9; 1 Cor 11:1).

Acts 20:18–20
You yourselves know how I lived among you the whole time from the first day that I set foot in Asia, serving the Lord with all humility and with tears and with trials that happened to me through the plots of the Jews; how I did not shrink from declaring to you anything that was profitable, and teaching you in public and from house to house,

166 Who should we disciple?

We should prioritize the discipleship of our family first, then members of our local church, and finally faithful Christians from other churches (Gal 6:10; 1 Tim 5:8; Titus 2:3-5).

Galatians 6:10
So then, as we have opportunity, let us do good to everyone, and especially to those who are of the household of faith.

WORSHIP

167 How can we worship God?

By glorifying and enjoying him in every-thing we do, offering our lives as living sacri-fices, holy and acceptable to God (Rom 12:1-2; 1 Cor 10:31).

1 Corinthians 10:31
So, whether you eat or drink, or whatever you do, do all to the glory of God.

168 Is attending a church service important to our worship?

Yes. We are commanded to regularly meet together for corporate worship. Some aspects of worship cannot be done apart from the gathering of the local church, such as the participation in the ordinances, and submitting to leadership (Heb 10:25; 13:15-17; Acts 20:7).

Hebrews 13:15–16
Through him then let us continually offer up a sacrifice of praise to God, that is, the fruit of lips that acknowledge his name. Do not neglect to do good and to share what you have, for such sacrifices are pleasing to God.

169 What are the essential elements of corporate worship?

Those elements that the New Testament explicitly commends, namely: **prayer, reading the Word, preaching the Word, singing, giving of offerings, baptism, and the Lord's Supper.** Although there should be uniformity in the elements included in corporate worship, various forms of each element are permitted (1 Cor 14:26, 40; 1 Tim 2:1-2; 1 Tim 4:13; Col 3:16).

1 Corinthians 14:40
But all things should be done decently and in order.

170 Why is singing an important element of worship?

As we sing, God delights in our praise, **we learn truths about God put to music and memory, and we teach those truths to one another.** Therefore, songs for corporate worship must be carefully chosen to reflect Biblical truth about God (Col 3:16; Ps 30:4).

Colossians 3:16
Let the word of Christ dwell in you richly, teaching and admonishing one another in all wisdom, singing psalms and hymns and spiritual songs, with thankfulness in your hearts to God.

171 Why is financial giving an important element of worship?

As we give of our finances, we recognize that all we have is from God, entrusted to us as a stewardship. **How we spend our money reflects the priorities of our hearts.** Therefore, we should contribute cheerfully, regularly, and sacrificially for the advancement of gospel ministry (Luke 12:15-21; 2 Cor 9:6-7; Ps 37:21).

2 Corinthians 9:7
Each one must give as he has decided in his heart, not reluctantly or under compulsion, for God loves a cheerful giver.

172 Why is serving an important aspect of worship?

As we serve, we give of our time, talents, and abilities for the strengthening of Christ's body rather than for our own good. Consequently, our serving must be varied according to the individual gifts each possess (1 Pet 4:10-11; Rom 12:5-8; 1 Cor 15:58).

1 Peter 4:10–11
As each has received a gift, use it to serve one another, as good stewards of God's varied grace: whoever speaks, as one who speaks oracles of God; whoever serves, as one who serves by the strength that God supplies—in order that in everything God may be glorified through Jesus Christ. To him belong glory and dominion forever and ever. Amen.

LAST THINGS

PERSONAL ESCHATOLOGY

173 Where do we go when we die?

Our bodies return to dust, and our soul remains conscious in an intermediate state. **If we belong to God, we go directly into the blessed presence of Christ with the redeemed; if we die in sin** and unbelief, **we go directly to hell with the damned** (2 Cor 5:8; Phil 1:23; Luke 16:19-31).

2 Corinthians 5:8
Yes, we are of good courage, and we would rather be away from the body and at home with the Lord.

174 Is it possible to be saved after death or purified from sin in purgatory?

No. It is appointed for us to die once and then face judgment, and there is no such place as purgatory (Heb 9:27; Luke 16:19-31; Matt 8:11-12).

Hebrews 9:27
And just as it is appointed for man to die once, and after that comes judgment,

175 Will our physical bodies ever live again?

Yes. All humanity will physically live again for eternity; both the redeemed and the damned will be resurrected (Dan 12:2; John 11:25-26; 1 Cor 15:42-44).

Daniel 12:2
And many of those who sleep in the dust of the earth shall awake, some to everlasting life, and some to shame and everlasting contempt.

176 Will all humanity be raised at the same time?

No. Blessed are the redeemed who partake in the first resurrection, when Christ returns to reign. **Cursed are the damned who partake in the second resurrection** and come before Christ at the Great White Throne Judgment (Rev 20:5-6, 11-13).

Revelation 20:6
Blessed and holy is the one who shares in the first resurrection! Over such the second death has no power, but they will be priests of God and of Christ, and they will reign with him for a thousand years.

177 What is hell and why is it to be feared?

Hell is the place of eternal, conscious torment for those not united to Christ by faith. It is **described as an unquenchable fire**, full of weeping and gnashing of teeth, where the dead will be joined by Satan and all the fallen angels (Matt 25:30, 41; Rev 14:9-11).

Matthew 25:41
Then he will say to those on his left, 'Depart from me, you cursed, into the eternal fire prepared for the devil and his angels.'

178 What is heaven and why is it our great source of hope?

Heaven is the place of eternal, conscious blessing for those united to Christ by faith. It is **described as a new creation**, a return to Edenic like blessings, with no sin, death, or disease, where in perfect bodies we will live with and enjoy God forever (Isa 65:17-18, 24-25; Rev 21:1-4).

Revelation 21:1
Then I saw a new heaven and a new earth, for the first heaven and the first earth had passed away, and the sea was no more.

179 Will the new heaven and new earth be like the first?

Yes. Part of Christ's work of redemption is to redeem every part of fallen creation and reverse the curse of Genesis 3. Therefore, creation waits eagerly to be renewed and will be like the first creation, without the effects of sin (Gen 3:17-19; Acts 3:21; Rom 8:18-23).

Romans 8:19–21
For the creation waits with eager longing for the revealing of the sons of God. For the creation was subjected to futility, not willingly, but because of him who subjected it, in hope that the creation itself will be set free from its bondage to corruption and obtain the freedom of the glory of the children of God.

180 Will we have things to do in the new earth?

Yes. There will still be distinct societies and nations in the new earth, and just as societies function here on earth, **we** too **will have certain jobs and tasks to perform for the good of the whole.** Similarly, there will be leisure and personal relationships to enjoy for all eternity (Rev 5:9-10; Rev 21:24-26; 22:3).

Revelation 21:24–25
By its light will the nations walk, and the kings of the earth will bring their glory into it, and its gates will never be shut by day—and there will be no night there.

181 Will everyone have equal roles in the new earth?

No. Distinct roles and responsibilities are not a result of the curse but God's created order. So, when we receive crowns and are judged according to our works, **we can expect that there will be diversity in the new earth, but it will never incite envy, greed, or sin of any kind** (1 Cor 9:24-25; 2 Cor 5:10; Matt 6:20).

2 Corinthians 5:10
For we must all appear before the judgment seat of Christ, so that each one may receive what is due for what he has done in the body, whether good or evil.

182 Will we be able to know our closest friends and family from this life in the new earth?

Yes. God created us to thrive in relationships, and we will be comforted knowing that we will see, know, and relate to **our loved ones again.** Our resurrected bodies and even personalities will still be distinct and recognizable, like Christ who rose before us (1 Thess 2:19-20; 4:16-18; 1 Cor 15:48-49).

1 Corinthians 15:48–49
As was the man of dust, so also are those who are of the dust, and as is the man of heaven, so also are those who are of heaven. Just as we have borne the image of the man of dust, we shall also bear the image of the man of heaven.

COSMIC ESCHATOLOGY

183 Where is Christ now?

After Christ's work of redemption was finished, **he rose physically from the dead**, ascended into heaven, **and is now seated at the right hand of the Father** (Col 3:1; Heb 10:12).

Hebrews 10:12
But when Christ had offered for all time a single sacrifice for sins, he sat down at the right hand of God,

184 What is Christ doing in heaven?

He upholds the universe and intercedes for us, granting us access to the Father (Heb 1:3; Rom 8:34).

Romans 8:34
Who is to condemn? Christ Jesus is the one who died—more than that, who was raised—who is at the right hand of God, who indeed is interceding for us.

185 When and how does Jesus say he will return?

Jesus will return personally, physically, obviously, and suddenly at a day and an hour known only to God. He will return as he ascended (Matt 24:36; 1 Thess 5:2; Acts 1:11-12; Zech 14:4; Luke 17:24).

Matthew 24:36
But concerning that day and hour no one knows, not even the angels of heaven, nor the Son, but the Father only.

186 Why are Christians "caught up" to meet Jesus in the air at his return?

Dispensational: **To deliver us from the wrath to come before the great seven-year tribulation**; also called the rapture, it is pretribulational. At this point the universal church is no more, and thus the great restraining presence of the Holy Spirit is set aside before the Day of the Lord (1 Thess 1:10; 4:16-18; Rev 3:10; 2 Thess 2:6-10).

✱ *Non-dispensational:* **To join the Lord in the air as he returns in judgment and victory** *over all his enemies (1 Thess 4:16-18; Luke 17:28-37; Rev 19:11-16).*

1 Thessalonians 1:10
and to wait for his Son from heaven, whom he raised from the dead, Jesus who delivers us from the wrath to come.

187 Is there a coming tribulation period and antichrist?

Yes. The Scriptures anticipate a great and terrible day of God's wrath and judgment on the earth. **Similarly**, even though many antichrists are already in the world, **a final antichrist is prophesied** (Isa 34:8; Matt 24:21; Rev 6-19; 1 John 2:18; 2 Thess 2:3-4).

Matthew 24:21
For then there will be great tribulation, such as has not been from the beginning of the world until now, no, and never will be.

188 What is the millennial kingdom?

Premillennial: **It is the literal, physical, and bodily reign of Christ in Jerusalem over the whole world lasting for one-thousand years.** Jesus ushers in the kingdom at his second coming where he destroys God's enemies, binds Satan, and sets up his reign. It is distinct from the new creation which comes after the millennium and is necessary to fulfill God's promises to national Israel (Rev 19-20; Isa 2:2-4; 65:19-20).

★ *Amillennial:* **It is not a literal kingdom, but rather refers to the spiritual kingdom at work in this present age through the gospel ministry of the church.** Satan is bound, thus enabling the advance of the gospel. When the fullness of time has come, Christ will return to judge the world and usher in the new creation (Rev 20; Luke 17:20-21).

Isaiah 2:2
It shall come to pass in the latter days that the mountain of the house of the LORD shall be established as the highest of the mountains, and shall be lifted up above the hills; and all the nations shall flow to it,

189 When will the final judgment take place?

At the Great White Throne, before the introduction of the new heavens and the new earth (Rev 20:11-15; Rom 2:5-8).

Revelation 20:11–12
Then I saw a great white throne and him who was seated on it. From his presence earth and sky fled away, and no place was found for them. And I saw the dead, great and small, standing before the throne, and books were opened. Then another book was opened, which is the book of life. And the dead were judged by what was written in the books, according to what they had done.

190 In light of all these future events, what is our great hope?

That death has lost its sting, that our Lord and Savior is certainly coming again soon, and **that we will perfectly glorify and enjoy God forever in his new creation. So, we say, "Amen. Come, Lord Jesus!"** (1 Cor 15:53-55; Rev 21:6-7; 22:20)

1 Corinthians 15:54b–55
Death is swallowed up in victory. O death, where is your victory? O death, where is your sting?

APPENDIX
BIBLICAL RATIONALE FOR USING A CATECHISM

Aristotle once said, "Happiness is the meaning and purpose of life, the whole aim and end of human existence." Not much has changed. We are bombarded with ads for virtual training sessions, tips to melt your fat away, and how to look like you're 20 again. Perhaps the problem of evil has been reduced to unwanted fat. Still, others don't look for happiness in physical fitness and healthy eating, but hope it's in achieving their career goals, wise investment strategies, or going on the ideal vacation. We all have things we live for; things we do that we hope will make us happy. And behind every ad, every self-help book, every Facebook post, we see a very important truth: we are hard-wired to search for meaning and joy in life.

But to have joy, we need direction. We need an aim. We need a life map to help us find our way. Sometimes we get whiplash chasing after the next wellness craze before we realize they all fail to deliver because they fail to place us on God's narrow path—the narrow path that leads to eternal life, godly wisdom, and true enjoyment. Now, if you've been a Christian for some time you're probably thinking, "Oh, I know how we're supposed to get on the narrow path: follow the Bible." True indeed! The Bible is a lamp unto our feet and a guide unto our paths, but there's something that the Bible teaches us that acts as our backbone, as our framework for keeping us on God's path—sound doctrine.

In the introduction we looked at several passages in the pastoral epistles that revealed sound doctrine isn't just for pastors and theologians, but is to be part of the diet of every Christian. It's our life map that helps us learn "to glorify God and enjoy him forever." A catechism then, acts as a vehicle for teaching sound doctrine, a skeleton that helps us rightly interpret the Bible and lead us to be truly happy, living as we were designed to live: in communion with the Creator. As we think about how the Bible speaks of the foundation of godly living, of how to find meaning in life, and how to discover sound doctrine, we must begin with the fear of God.

The Foundation of Sound Doctrine: Fear God

Proverbs is abundantly clear: "The fear of the Lord is the beginning of wisdom" (Prov 1:7; 9:10). But without knowing God and having a framework for following his will, it is impossible to fear, worship, and honor God with your life. Therefore, to establish a framework for understanding God is paramount.

It is entirely too common to fear an imagined god and not fear the one true and living God. In 21st century America, most want a god who is there for them when they want him, loves them unconditionally, and simply winks at their indiscretions. This false god is nothing more than an idol made up in the minds of the unregenerate and tragically perpetuated and peddled in some popular pulpits. Genuine fear of this god is impossible. Knowledge of him comes from within, not the revealed Word.

Instead, Christians must turn to God's Word where they discover the beginning of wisdom has always been knowing and fearing God. The fool in Proverbs refuses to learn and fear God. Whereas the wise son is constantly learning and building upon his sure foundation—the fear of God.

Proverbs 1-9 is written to instruct a young man in the way he should go by helping him "to know wisdom and instruction, to understand words of insight" (Prov 1:2), and to grasp who God is and what it looks like to fear him (Prov 1:7). This falls on parents and spiritual mothers and fathers to help younger believers grasp and apply the wisdom that comes from God.[1] Repeatedly, Solomon calls his son to learn, memorize, and apply the knowledge and fear of God to all of life while at the same time warning him of the terrible consequences of neglecting his wisdom. To walk on the path of wisdom and fear of God, his son must first make sure he has left the ways of the simple.

Have you Left the Simple Ways?

Leave your simple ways, and live,
And walk in the way of insight. (Prov 9:6)

Another word for the *simple* is *gullible*—one who is easily convinced by every passing trend and popular sentiment. The starting point of growing in sound doctrine is to recognize folly as folly and aim for the commendation of God, not self. It is to let God be the arbiter of truth, not what seems reasonable to the world.

American founding father Thomas Jefferson was one of history's most notable skeptics. He famously cut the miracles out of the gospel accounts, leaving only the sayings of Jesus that he considered pertinent to the day. He was also a vocal critic of the doctrine of the Trinity which he attributed to a deformed myth. He blamed theologians for its development, writing to a friend in February 1821, "The religion-builders have so distorted and deformed the doctrines of Jesus, so muffled them in mysticisms, fancies and falsehoods ... as to shock reasonable thinkers." He was almost giddy, "with great pleasure at the progress of reason [that would] ... do away with the incomprehensible jargon of the Trinity."[2]

Not much has changed today as many assume the Bible to be riddled with myths and fanciful ideas. But to fear God must begin with repentance— to leave the simple ways (the Jeffersonian way of thinking) and turn towards trusting that when God speaks in his Word, he does not stutter. No longer can man be judge over what God says but must always be subject to his Creator. So, Solomon is clear that the fear of God must begin with leaving the simple ways. Further, if you are serious about leaving the simple ways, you must be willing to conform your life and doctrine to the truths God has revealed.

Are you Confrontable with God's Truth?

Whoever corrects a scoffer gets himself abuse,
and he who reproves a wicked man incurs injury.
Do not reprove a scoffer, or he will hate you;
reprove a wise man, and he will love you.
Give instruction to a wise man, and he will be still wiser;
teach a righteous man, and he will increase in learning.
(Prov 9:7-9)

In three parallel statements the wicked, scoffing son refuses to learn; even causing injury on any who would dare help, whereas the wise son is thrice praised for being, of all things, confrontable. The scoffer is unconcerned with God and his holy character. Instead, he desires to be the final authority of what is true. But the wise son is interested in learning at the fountain of all wisdom—the fear of God. The fear of God can only be learned by the one who recognizes the simple paths previously traveled, desires to get off, and then is open to ongoing correction. The pursuit of sound doctrine is a whole-life pursuit and at many points Christians must be open to conform their ideas about God to God's ideas about God. Thus, the fear of God is the beginning and the end of this process.

Do you Know God Well Enough to Fear Him?

The fear of the LORD is the beginning of wisdom,
and the knowledge of the Holy One is insight.
(Prov 9:10)

The foundation of all wisdom, of all sound doctrine, and of all catechisms, must be the knowledge and fear of God. For it is only when God is known that men can know themselves. Only when we grasp our sinfulness before a holy God and great dependence upon God for all of life, can we be able to grow like the wise son of Proverbs 9. Note the parallel in verse 10, for to *fear* God is to *know* God. So, any knowledge of God that does not lead to an appropriate, reverential fear is not true knowledge.

There is a profound sense of awe that parents are to instill in their children when they teach them about the holy God. Therefore, they ought to choose their words carefully. Part of what makes a catechism so helpful is that it contains those carefully crafted words that lead to both knowing and fearing God. Proverbs does not promote a flippant exploration of God within a child's own imagination. Rather, Solomon provided a careful expression of God that is taught and learned, leading the wise son to fear him.

Additionally, part of knowing and fearing God is to internalize those truths. Memorization allows the wise son to hold them deep within his heart. Proverbs 4:20-23 makes this point explicit.

My son, be attentive to my words;
incline your ear to my sayings.
Let them not escape from your sight;
keep them within your heart.
For they are life to those who find them,
healing to their entire body.
Keep your heart with all vigilance,
for from it flow the springs of life. (Prov 4:20-23)[3]

Committing truths to memory is a powerful tool that God frequently encourages his people to employ (cf. Deut 11:18; Josh 1:8; Pss 37:31; 119:9, 11; Col 3:16). Proverbs 4:21 expands the call to memorize by telling us to "keep them within your heart." This is not a pursuit of knowledge for knowledge's sake but an eager and diligent pursuit of God's wisdom that is so carefully learned it remains within, intimately accessible at any moment. And so, Solomon encouraged his son to stay "attentive," to "incline 'his' ear," to "let them not escape" (Prov 4:20-21). The effort to walk in God's wisdom includes constant attention and care to lean into God's truths, revisiting the realities learned and memorized in the past, because they have the tendency to flit and flutter out of the heart. But when the foundational knowledge of God, and thus the fear of God, takes root within, it produces a life-giving spring that keeps the wise son on the straight and narrow (Prov 4:23).

When the righteous man knows the fear of God it is because he respects the holiness of God, which in turn directs his ways toward what pleases God. That is how the fear of God becomes the foundation of sound doctrine and thus sound living. Children up through adults ought to have a consistent framework for understanding who God is and what he requires learned and guarded within their heart. That way, their paths will remain straight—following and fearing their Creator. A catechism, providing this framework of knowing and fearing God, is an excellent starting point for training up Christians to walk on the narrow path that leads to eternal life.

The Generational Effect of Sound Doctrine: Love for God

There are times in history when generational divides seem to widen. Nineteen-sixties America, as the Baby Boomers came of age, was such a time. Events like Woodstock and the Vietnam War protests are permanently etched in the minds of Americans. "Love" and "Peace" were trumpeted on banners, emblazoned on clothing, or simply painted on bodies. But these intangible realities didn't materialize simply by speaking them loud enough. Far better is God's solution to promote a love that lasts and bring generations together: sound doctrine.

In the short epistle of 2 John, the apostle of love speaks of his affection for the elect lady and her children, as a "love in truth." These twin ideas are repeated, indicating the glue of generational affection is truth, or sound doctrine. Thus, to learn sound doctrine is to simultaneously grow in love for God and love for others. For the more one knows God, the easier it is to pursue the highest of all the commands, "You shall love the Lord your God with all your heart and with all your soul and with all your strength and with all your mind, and your neighbor as yourself." (Luke 10:27) Knowing sound doctrine propels our love, like wind in a sail.

To go sailing is to be dependent on the wind. That is why 300 years ago sailors would dread most of all the dead spots in the ocean where the wind stopped, sometimes for months at a time. Even the strong could die if God didn't bring the wind. Something bigger and stronger than the ship had to fill the sails and push the boat along. Many prefer to think of love, like the wind, as uncontrollable. It comes and goes like "a whimsical muse. If the muse strikes us, we're inspired. If not, we're indifferent."[4]

But the greatest commandment, first explicitly commanded in Deuteronomy 6:5, is a command to love God. To love God does not mean to follow affections wherever they might lead, but instead, to steadfastly aim to know, fear, and love God always and in all things. Therefore, sound doctrine is the wind that fills the sails of the faithful, helping them learn to love God.

Internally Learn Sound Doctrine

You shall love the LORD your God with all your heart and with all your soul and with all your might. And these words that I command you today shall be on your heart. (Deut 6:5-6)

Love is not passive. It is not something that just happens to someone. Love is an attitude adopted when an individual personally knows the beauty of God's love. "In this is love, not that we have loved God but that he loved us." (1 John 4:10) Therefore, Moses only gave the command to love after his commands to listen to, know, and fear God. The believer's love for God is fundamentally responsive to God's prior love for us. And yet one's love for God is far more than a feeling. It is marked by faithful obedience and continual pursuit of God. So, in Deuteronomy the verb "to love" does not simply mean an emotional attachment but to "act lovingly."[5]

Only those who know sound doctrine can pursue God with such a whole-hearted zeal—a zeal which Moses described as loving God "with all your heart and with all your soul and with all your might" (Deut 6:5). Followers of Yahweh should pursue loving God with the whole person. So, love ought to come from the "heart" (that is, the volitional part of man—the mind or intellect), the "soul" (the immaterial part of man), and with all "strength" (the physical side).[6] Consequently, all the person, in all possible divisions, is to be committed to pursuing, loving, and obeying God.

Many distractions vie for our affections, but God alone is worth loving for all eternity. Benefits abound for those who've learned such sound doctrine through a carefully crafted catechism. Affections are roused for God when we know him and the depth of his love for us. Catechisms are an excellent tool for keeping "these words… on your heart" (Deut 6:6), and for having readily available truths about God to help guide conversations with future generations.

Regularly Talk About Sound Doctrine

You shall teach them diligently to your children, and shall talk of them when you sit in your house, and when you walk by the way, and when you lie down, and when you rise. You shall bind them as a sign on your hand, and they shall be as frontlets between your eyes. You shall write them on the doorposts of your house and on your gates. (Deut 6:7-9)

Here is the essence why, for many centuries, the church has employed a catechism in maintaining generational faithfulness: God wants who he is and what he commands to be orally learned, repeated, and clearly explained in many different settings. The Hebrew word translated "teach them diligently," is rich with implications for catechesis. First, its primary idea is to learn by repetition.[7] It is not an idea taught once and hoped to take root. The doctrines God has preserved in his Word are to be poured over again and again, carefully guarded, taught, and learned. As a seminary professor of mine repeatedly told our class, "Repetition is the key to learning, and the key to learning is …" pausing for dramatic effect and waiting for the class to finish the statement. The idea of careful repetition comes directly from the Lord and is built into the language used to encourage us to "diligently teach" the knowledge, fear, and love of God. Therefore, a carefully crafted catechism used to train generations of Christians ought to be repeated frequently in the life of the church.

Second, the Hebrew word for "teach them diligently," can also mean to sharpen and even to pierce.[8] When applied metaphorically, it "suggests teaching in such a way as to make a deep impression upon the learner," to make them equipped for any and every situation.[9] That's why a good catechism will not only ground the Christian in the basis of the gospel message but include a base for all theology—all the concepts, truths, and sound doctrines found in the word of God. As J.I. Packer once asked, "How was such deep and impressive teaching to be done? It would need to be intentional, multisensory, and constant."[10] And so Moses instructed the people to that end.

Considering the quartet of occasions when teaching should take place in the rest of verse 7, Moses intended instruction of God's ways to be constant.

It didn't matter if it was the early morning or late in the evening. It didn't matter if work, travel, or pleasure were at hand. God's ways were to be constantly before the men and women of God in every generation. Followers of Yahweh were to anticipate interpreting all of life through the grid of what they knew and believed to be true about God and his will for their lives.

Further, training in the ways of God ought to be multisensory and intentional, seen in the quartet of locations mentioned in verses 8 and 9. "On your hand, and ... as frontlets between your eyes," (or forehead), signifies that all a person does with his hands or thinks with his head must be filtered through the commands of God. After all, are not the hands and forehead the most used and visible parts of the body? Similarly, "doorposts" and "gates" affirm an intentional, all encompassing, multisensory approach to learning. The doorposts were the entrance into a family home and the gates the entrance into the city.[11] So as families left and returned through the doors of their family home, they should remember these truths about God. As the community left and returned through the gates of the city, the realities of who God is and what he requires should be ever before the whole community.[12]

To have such a pervasive worldview, the realities that God desires for his people to pass on to the next generation must be both accurate and readily accessible. For as important as it is to have excellent systematic theologies, carrying a thousand-page tome around is impractical. But a learned catechism is a great starting point for the type of questions that permeate all of life that must be answered from a thoroughly Christian worldview.

The only way we can hope to have this pervasive, God-centered approach to life is to have his truth internalized. That's why learning a catechism has proven so helpful in times past and is such a vital practice to adopt again into the life of the church. A well-crafted catechism can help clearly define who God is and the essence of sin. It can give a healthy sense of fear for the Creator, while at the same time engendering a devoted love towards him as Savior. Applying the Christian faith to all of life is also easier with a catechism as it will not only teach Christians to know doctrines and facts but also the right questions to ask. This skill is invaluable in taking truths of God and applying it to every situation. Deuteronomy 6 is an early commendation by God himself, of some of the hallmarks of catechetical learning. But there is a third benefit of sound doctrine that the Scriptures reveal to be indispensable: discernment.

The Protection of Sound Doctrine: Discernment

Theological error today seems to be as prevalent as ever. Paul's instruction to Timothy is timeless: inoculate the church against all sorts of false teaching by training everyone to know the good doctrines of the faith (1 Tim 4:1-11). What better way to deposit truth in God's people than through robust theological frameworks in the form of a catechism? Though a catechism is not the only application of this text, I believe learning a catechism to be as sure a foundation as any in the training of saints to recognize and flee error—to grow in discernment.

In describing the weakness of this current generation, Albert Mohler describes the American church as "missing the art of evangelical discernment."[13] With evangelicalism enduring generations of watered-down preaching, philosophy of ministries aimed at drawing the biggest crowds, and many Christian ministries highly concerned with offending as few as possible, it is not surprising that discernment is lacking among so many in the pews. Paul's remedy to a lack of discernment, he tells Timothy, is to teach sound doctrine.

Know Sound Doctrine to Discern Lies

If you put these things before the brothers, you will be a good servant of Christ Jesus, being trained in the words of the faith and of the good doctrine that you have followed. Have nothing to do with irreverent, silly myths. (1 Tim 4:6-7a)

Putting truth "before the brothers" includes, in the context of this passage, the public reading and preaching of the Scriptures (1 Tim 4:13). But it is important to note that it isn't just the words of Scriptures that are placed before the church. Paul details Christian training to include "words of the faith" and words "of the good doctrine." The words of course include Scriptures, but likely much more. For it is not just "words of the faith" (often a summary for the basics of the gospel message), but words of "good doctrine" (or sound doctrine), to which the apostle refers.[14] Some of the most enduring doctrinal statements of truth have been hymns, creeds, and catechetical formulations; enduring because these forms are designed to be memorized and thus permeate the heart in a unique way. Paul is explicit, Scripture alone is the source of authority, but doctrine derived from the Scriptures is profitable—especially for fighting lies.

It's fascinating (comical at times, but profound at others), to watch a four-year-old think and process truth. As our family was traveling home after ministering in a predominately Muslim community, I talked about how Muslims don't believe that Jesus or the Holy Spirit are, in any sense, God. So, I asked my four-year-old daughter if she thought that was right. She perked right up and said in the words of her catechism, "The Holy Spirit is God, coeternal with the Father and the Son."

It always becomes easier to apply theological knowledge when you have the scaffolding of accurate doctrines built in your mind. That was Paul's point, as he commanded, "have nothing to do with irreverent, silly myths." Warnings are heeded only by those who know sound doctrine well enough to recognize truth from error. But the theological framework that is so important in defending the faith does not come easily.

Train Hard in Sound Doctrine to be Godly

Rather train yourself for godliness; for while bodily training is of some value, godliness is of value in every way, as it holds promise for the present life and also for the life to come. The saying is trustworthy and deserving of full acceptance. For to this end we toil and strive, because we have our hope set on the living God, who is the Savior of all people, especially of those who believe. (1 Tim 4:7b-10)

Compared to false teaching, which Paul calls "silly" and vacuous (v.7a), the Word of God and the doctrines derived from it are of eternal value (vv.7b-8). Paul makes a natural comparison for the body-centered, fitness culture of ancient Ephesus. With their highly prized athletic achievements and emphasis on physical fitness, many in 21st century America can relate. Scores of people religiously spend time in gyms, small fortunes on workout equipment, and carefully count every calorie. But as helpful as physical fitness can be, training in godliness and sound doctrine is far more valuable. What an indictment that many in the church do not pursue sound doctrine with the same zeal as physical fitness. "For while bodily training is of some value, godliness is of value in every way" (v.8).

Considering the great worth of sound doctrine, Paul says Christians are to "toil and strive" after it (v.10). We should work so hard as to grow weary and tired, even fighting for it.[15] Growth in godliness does not happen passively but requires full engagement of the mind, body, and soul applied in a fight that has eternal ramifications. (That sounds a lot like Deuteronomy 6:5 to me.) So, Paul compelled Timothy:

Command and teach these things. (1 Tim 4:11)

Conclusion

A catechism is a valuable and scripturally warranted aid for the whole church. As Paul clarified for Timothy, not only should elders read and explain the text of Scriptures, but various tools should also be used to implant Scriptural truths and accurate doctrines within the hearts and minds of every Christian. For generations, the church has seen a good catechism as essential to this end.

A Catechism for Christian Growth is specifically designed to fit into a variety of settings in the Christian life. It helps parents shepherd their children, new converts understand the fundamentals of the faith, and entire congregations learn sound doctrine. It is a succinct yet systematic scaffolding upon which Christians can fortify their faith and defend against all sorts of heresy. But defense is hardly the only benefit of catechesis, for it will also engender a deep and abiding reverence for the Creator (Prov 4:20-27) and a warmth of affection for God as Christians rest in his electing love (Deut 6:5-9). The theological framework of a catechism follows the catechumen into the study informing her times of devotion and private worship; it follows her into the marketplace to understand how a simple job can be done for the glory of God; it follows her into the home where she is able to self-diagnose problems within her marriage and between her children according to clear biblical principles; and it follows her into the pew to inform her worship and grow her devotion for her Lord and Savior. The good doctrines taught in a catechism can have a profound impact on all of life, as Christians realize their "hope is set on the living God, who is the Savior of all" (1 Tim 4:10b).

---

[1] Bruce K. Waltke, *The Book of Proverbs, Chapters 1-15,* NICOT (Grand Rapids: Wm. B. Eerdmans, 2004), 12. That parents are to be intimately involved in instructing their children in the wisdom of God, is repeated throughout chapters 1-9. Waltke notes it is the father, in particular, in Proverbs that must be the protector and purveyor of God's wisdom.

[2] Thomas Jefferson, "From Thomas Jefferson to Timothy Pickering, 27 February 1821," *Founders Online,* National Archives, https://founders.archives.gov/documents/Jefferson/98-01-02-1870.

[3] Verse 22 is Longman's translation. Tremper Longman, III, Proverbs, Baker Commentary on the Old Testament Wisdom and Psalms (Grand Rapids: Baker Academic, 2006), 153.

[4] Bobby Jamieson, *Sound Doctrine* (Wheaton, IL: Crossway, 2013), 64.

[5] Tigay notes that "Hebrew verbs for feelings (like love), can refer as well to actions" that express that feeling. Thus, in the context of Israel being a suzerain of sorts, they are also to "act loyally to him." Jeffrey H. Tigay, *Deuteronomy*, JPSTC (Philadelphia: Jewish Publication Society, 1996), 77. See also Robert L. Alden, *"ahar,"* in TWOT, ed. R. Laird Harris, Gleason L. Archer, and Bruce K. Waltke, 1:14-15 (Chicago: Moody Press, 1980), 14.

[6] Eugine H. Merrill, *Deuteronomy*, NAC (Nashville: Holman Reference, 1994), 164. Interesting to note that when Jesus quotes this passage in Luke 10:27, he adds the word "mind," no doubt adding that word simply because it falls within the rich semantic range of the Hebrew word, *livav*.

[7] Ludwig Koehler and Walter Baumgartner, eds. *HALOT*, revised by Walter Baumgartner and Johann Jakob Stamm, trans. and ed. M. E. J. Richardson (Leiden: E. J. Brill, 1994), 4:1606-07; Tigay, *Deuteronomy*, 78.

[8] *HALOT*, 4:1606.

[9] J. I. Packer and Gary A. Parrett, *Grounded in the Gospel: Building Believers the Old-Fashioned Way* (Grand Rapids: Baker Books, 2010), 34.

[10] Packer and Parrett, *Grounded in the Gospel*, 34.

[11] Tigay, *Deuteronomy*, 79.

[12] I follow Merrill in the interpretation of these commands as representative of what it means to teach God's ways in all of life. The Jewish commentator Tigay implies that they were meant to be taken literally and draws the connection to Jewish practices carried out today of wrapping a leather pouch with the words contained within on one's hand and forehead. Merrill, *Deuteronomy*, 167-168; Tigay, *Deuteronomy*, 78-79.

[13] R. Albert Mohler, "The Shack — The Missing Art of Evangelical Discernment," *AlbertMohler.com,* March 7, 2017, https://albertmohler.com/2017/03/06/shack-missing-art-evangelical-discernment/. This article was first published in 2010 when *The Shack*, was on the New York Times Best seller lists while being marketed as Christian fiction.

[14] George W. Knight III, *The Pastoral Epistles,* NIGTC (Grand Rapids: Wm. B. Eerdmans Publishing, 1992), 194; William D. Mounce, *Pastoral Epistles*, WBC (Nashville: Thomas Nelson, 2000), 249. Mounce and Knight aptly note that *logois* is qualified by two genitives, "of the faith and of the good doctrine." Hendriksen writes, "The apostle may be thinking of certain summaries of doctrine which, in the form of current reliable sayings and other fixed formulations of truth, could be considered good spiritual nourishment." William Hendriksen, *Thessalonians, Timothy, and Titus,* NTC (Grand Rapids: Baker, 1979), 149.

[15] Walter Bauer, W. F. Arndt, F. W. Gingrich, and F. W. Danker, *A Greek-English Lexicon of the New Testament and other Early Christian Literature*, 3rd ed., ed. F. W. Danker (Chicago: The University of Chicago Press, 2000), 558, 17.

ANNOTATED BIBLIOGRAPHY

Hammett   John S. Hammett, *Biblical Foundations for Baptist Churches: A Contemporary Ecclesi-ology*, 2nd ed. (Grand Rapids: Kregel Academic, 2019). Monograph on ecclesiology.

Allison   Gregg R. Allison, *50 Core Truths of the Christian Faith* (Grand Rapids: Baker Books, 2018). Short systematic theology.

DC   Brian Dembowczyk, *Cornerstones Parent Guide, 200 Questions and Answers to Teach Truth* (Nashville: B&H Publishing Group, 2018). Original catechism.

NCC   Redeemer Presbyterian Church, *The New City Catechism,* The Gospel Coalition (Wheaton, IL: Crossway, 2017). Shortened and revised Heidelberg.

Jamison   Bobby Jamieson, *Understanding Baptism,* Church Basics Series (Nashville: B&H Publishing Group, 2016). Short book for laity.

Piper   John Piper, "What is Sin? The Essence and Root of All Sinning," *Desiring God Blog,* February 2, 2015, https://www.desiringgod.org/messages/what-is-sin-the-essence-and-root-of-all-sinning. Transcribed sermon.

Whitney   Donald S. Whitney, Praying the Bible (Wheaton: Crossway, 2015). Short book for laity.

Truth: 78   Sally Michael, *My Purpose Will Stand: A Study for Children on the Providence of God* (Mendota Heights, MN: Truth78, 2013). Sunday school curriculum.

FOF   Grace Community Church, *Fundamentals of the Faith* (Chicago: Moody Publishers, 2009). Curriculum for new Christians developed by Grace Community Church, Sun Valley, CA.

BFM 2000   Douglas K. Blount and Joseph D. Wooddell, eds. *The Baptist Faith and Message 2000: Critical Issues in America's Largest Protestant Denomination* (Lanham, MD: Rowman & Littlefield Publishers, 2007). Monograph on the history of the Southern Baptist Convention's confession of faith. Only the *Baptist Faith and Message 2000* is cited.

Alcorn   Randy Alcorn, *Heaven* (Carol Stream, IL: Tyndale House Publishers, 2004). Monograph on history, much of which is organized into questions and answers.

BTB   John A. Broadus, *A Catechism of Bible Teaching* (Nashville: Sunday School Board of the Southern Baptist Convention, 1892). Original catechism.

BDB   James P. Boyce, *A Brief Catechism of Bible Doctrine* (Louisville: Caperton & Cates Publishers, 1878). Original catechism.

SC   C. H. Spurgeon and T. T. Eaton, *A Baptist Catechism with Proofs* (Louisville: Baptist Book, 1898). Revised Westminster/Keach, originally published in 1855.

CGB   *Catechism for Girls and Boys,* in Thomas J. Nettles Teaching Truth, Training Hearts: The Study of Catechisms in Baptist Life (Cape Coral, FL: Founders Press, 2017). Simplified Westminster/Keach, originally published 1798.

KBC   Benjamin Keach, *The Baptist Catechism; Commonly Called Keach's Catechism* (Philadelphia: American Baptist Publication Society, 1813). Revised Westminster, originally published 1693.

OC   Hercules Collins, *An Orthodox Catechism: Being the Sum of Christian Religion, Contained in the Law and Gospel,* ed. Michael A. G. Haykin and G. Stephen Weaver, Jr. (Palmdale, CA: Reformed Baptist Academic Press, 2014). Revised Heidelberg, originally published 1680.

CATECHISM NOTES

All citations below indicate a reference to the source, not a full reproduction of the question and/or answer. A few phrases are quotes of the works cited, but in order to keep the catechism more readable I chose to eliminate quotation marks and use them only for the direct quotation of Scriptures.

1.	SC 1	63.	OC 13	136.	OC 94
2.	OC 1, NCC 1	64.	NCC 19	138.	Jamieson, 6
9.	DC	67.	NCC 20	139.	OC 77, BTB
22.	KBC 7, NCC 2	68.	NCC 21	140.	BTB
23.	SC 5	70.	OC 17	141.	KBC 99
24.	KBC 9	74.	SC 22	144.	NCC 47
27.	Allison, 90	75.	CGB 84-85	145.	KBC 103, BTB
33.	DC	76.	CGB 86-87	146.	Hammett, 323-26
38.	SC 9	77.	CGB 88-89	149.	KBC 105
41.	*Truth:* 78	79.	NCC 26	152.	KBC 106, Whitney, 32
42.	OC 27	83.	BTB	155.	OC 142
43.	KBC 13	84.	NCC 36	156.	KBC 95
51.	CGB 27	86.	NCC 37	159.	DC
53.	NCC 6	89.	Allison, 196-97	160.	FOF 11
54.	OC 4	103.	NCC 30	171.	BFM 2000
58.	NCC 13	106.	BTB	173.	CGB 140
59.	NCC 15	109.	NCC 32	175.	BTB
60.	Piper	113.	NCC 33	181.	Alcorn, 369
61.	NCC 17	135.	OC 92		

SCRIPTURE INDEX

www.ingramcontent.com/pod-product-compliance
Lightning Source LLC
Chambersburg PA
CBHW060134100426
42744CB00007B/787